As a composer, conductor, educator, editor, and someone who has had many other musical jobs (as all musicians have), I am so inspired and encouraged by the wisdom and practicality shared in this wonderful book by Patricia Bourne. From the preface to the final summary, the text reflects Patty and her teaching experience as well as her personal character—enlightening, funny, informative, casual, friendly. It's like talking with your best friend about ideas, stories, problems, and solutions in the comfort of a big easy chair!

Patty gives the reader goals, expectations, teaching techniques, and so many "ah-ha!" moments in every chapter. I love and admire her "it's not what will we teach, but what will they learn" approach and student-first commitment. I applaud her belief that everyone should enjoy music and that we are to create an atmosphere of learning if we are going to be successful. She informs the reader using her experiences and breaks it all down so that a wealth of information is easy to understand and incorporate. It is truly motivating for me to read. I think I've highlighted most of the book for my own purposes!

I realize this book is designed to help the general music teacher enter the world of choral teaching and performance, however this passionate and compassionate text is perfect for the graduating music educator, the teacher changing jobs or level of teaching, and the well-experienced educator who needs a refresher course that includes a B-12 shot of creativity, as well as the person who just needs to focus on some simple goals for a program that might have a bit of chaos within it. I think we've all been there! What a treasure this book is, and a valuable resource to reach for again and again.

—*Greg Gilpin*
Someone who adores Patty and is lucky to now have this resource
Indianapolis, Indiana

As a Fine and Performing Arts Coordinator, choral director, and music educator of 35 years, it is a unique honor to recommend this wonderful book written by Patricia Bourne, who attended and graduated from our school district. She was an outstanding student and is now an outstanding educator in her own right. We are proud to have played some small part in her development and applaud her as the teacher of teachers that she has become.

In this book, Patricia helps unlock the keys to excellent elementary choral programs, giving reference and insight into:

- Teacher expectations, organization, and preparation
- Belief in the innate abilities of *all* children
- Rapport and human connectivity with *all* stakeholders

Reward your students and your music program by utilizing this insightful text.

—*Julie Ann White*
Fine Arts Coordinator, Owensboro Public Schools
Owensboro, Kentucky

If as a beginning teacher I had read this book, it surely would have compelled me to start a choir! Dr. Bourne has provided an inspiring model for the elementary school chorus. Indeed her book delivers practical ideas and procedures for developing a choral program that will be very useful for experienced as well as novice teachers. The book gives insights into Dr. Bourne's practice that make transparent the underlying tenets of her approach—tenets that transcend her musical goals. Certainly, her desire that her students (and those of the reader) have a rich and meaningful musical experience springs off each page, but of equal importance is that each singer's role in the choir translates into responsible community membership and respectful citizenship. Because Dr. Bourne's choral model offers more than excellent performance, it is also a recipe for gaining the support of parents, faculty and administrators. This book is more than a manual on the school choir—it is a beautiful self-portrait of a master teacher.

My congratulations to you!

—Mary Goetze
Professor Emeritus, Jacobs School of Music
Indiana University
Bloomington, Indiana

Patricia Bourne's *Inside the Elementary School Chorus* is an engaging and delightful book that is packed with useful information delivered in a humorous manner. A blueprint for success for directors of any children's chorus, Patty incorporates real-life examples from her teaching career to illustrate her beliefs. The result is a revealing and well-organized look at the step-by-step processes of a true master teacher. While reading, I found that Patty was answering my next question even before it had been fully formed in my head!

This is a wonderful resource for teachers in any stage of their career, as Patty reiterates the basics while encouraging all teachers to rise to their very best and expect high standards both in behavior as well as musically: "The best conducting skills in the world will not mean a thing if the classroom or rehearsal is a place where chaos reigns...the children's choir director hones skills that provide their choristers with effective sequential instruction, quality repertoire that fits the group, and a genuine interest in establishing a musical community that has meaning and purpose to everyone involved."

After reading this book, I simply couldn't wait to get back to my choir! Above all, it helped me believe that I can do it! I can be the director of a successful and inspiring children's chorus. And you can too.

—Carinn Ormson
National Board Certified Teacher
Music Specialist, Endeavour Elementary
Vancouver, Washington

Patricia Bourne has made an outstanding contribution to the music education profession by writing *Inside the Elementary School Chorus: Instructional Techniques for the Non-Select Children Chorus*. In the past, elementary music teachers conducting (teaching!) the elementary chorus have had to rely on choral texts that are written for middle school, high school, college or professional, or select treble choruses. Now there is a text that deals with the real world that elementary teachers find themselves in every day.

As with other music education texts and instructional books, many people can write these books, but the best books come from authors with practical, hands-on experience. Patty is the epitome of that author so provides pragmatic and tested strategies for every facet of making non-select elementary choruses look, act, and sound great. From recruiting (reaching out, not just having the students come to you) to fun ways to get kids excited to identifying personalities and developmental tendencies to warm-ups to dealing with parents to programming to budget...*it is in this book!* In addition, the reference section is a definitive list of additional resources for those readers wanting more.

This book is *the* book for elementary teachers working with choirs within their school. As important as general music is in K–12 education, we all know that there is no greater feeling (for students, teachers, and parents) than singing quality literature at the highest level of choral musicianship. This *can* happen at the elementary level and within the school setting, and Patty Bourne's book is a pedagogical guide to getting you there. Thank you Patty and Heritage Music Press for this outstanding resource!

—Russell L. Robinson, Ph.D.
Professor of Music and Head, Music Education
University of Florida
Gainesville, Florida

Inside the Elementary School Chorus

Instructional Techniques for the Non-Select Children's Chorus

Patricia Bourne

HERITAGE MUSIC PRESS

a Lorenz company • www.lorenz.com

Editors: Mary Lynn Lightfoot and Kris Kropff
Book Design: Digital Dynamite, Inc.
Cover Design: Patti Jeffers

Photos courtesy of Mark Mayberry. Used by permission.

Permissions and credits for the songs heard on the DVD are
listed on pages 156–157.

Heritage Music Press
A division of The Lorenz Corporation
P.O. Box 802
Dayton, OH 45401-0802
www.lorenz.com

Printed in the United States of America

ISBN: 978-1-4291-0010-6

Contents

Preface

I distinctly remember the first time I attended a performance of a children's chorus that rivaled the musicianship of any adult choral group I'd previously heard. The Glen Ellyn Children's Chorus, under the direction of past director Doreen Rao, performed for the participants of a national music educators conference, delighting the audience with their heightened level of musicianship, their approach to intricate and sophisticated choral repertoire, and the ease and confidence projected while singing in front of hundreds of music educators.

It was a sound I'd not heard before. How was it possible for young people (aged approximately 9–13) to sing like this? I was still in my first few years as an elementary music teacher and, while my students sang well, they/we didn't come close to the level of musicianship and professionalism projected by this professional children's choral group.

I was intrigued, curious, and somewhat puzzled. If this was the model and benchmark for children's choirs, was it possible for *my* students to pursue that standard? Was it possible for regular intermediate elementary students to sing in a school-sponsored choral ensemble with this level of expertise and musicianship? Furthermore, was it possible for me, their general music teacher, to coordinate and conduct with the skills necessary to approach anything like what I'd heard?

Curiosity (and the desire to find a meaningful research topic for graduate studies) led to an in-depth investigation of what Dr. Rao and other directors of outstanding children's choirs do to develop choral ensembles of extraordinary quality. I had the great fortune of observing the rehearsals of six directors from multiple regions of the country, representing both professional-level choruses and school-sponsored ensembles. In addition, I talked with each at length about his or her process for soliciting and choosing chorus members, what repertoire was selected and how it was sequenced for careful instruction, how and when rehearsals occurred, where performances took place, and whether a formula existed for guiding children toward extraordinary choral experiences.

These directors openly shared their philosophies, their instructional tips, and, most importantly, their passion and conviction that all children have the capacity for profound musical experiences. Watching these masters work was a unique and gratifying experience and led to years of honing my skills as general music teacher and choral director. Each of these individuals believed that children could achieve mastery in the skills of singing if provided appropriate instruction, quality repertoire, and guidance toward that end. The directors concurred with Kodály's statement, "Teach music and singing to children in such a way that it is not torture but a joy for the pupil: instill a thirst for finer music in him, a thirst which will last a lifetime."[1]

In my early years of teaching, I believed my students were far more capable than I'd given them credit for. The truth? Their limitations were a reflection of my own limitations as teacher and director. It was time to begin looking at my preparation, knowledge, and skills so that my students might achieve what they were so very capable of. Perhaps they would not sound like a professional, auditioned children's chorus, but they certainly could sing better with purposeful instruction.

In our elementary schools, general music teachers (like me) often serve as directors of their choirs. Unlike the community-based choirs I observed, members of the ensemble directed by a school's general music teacher are drawn from one's own students. They are as diverse as the typical American public school classroom, with a heterogeneous mix of cognitive, physical, and behavioral capabilities. Rehearsals are held when it best fits the school's daily or weekly schedule. Additional personnel, like accompanists, tend to be scarce. Budgets are limited, as is time.

Regardless of obstacles, circumstances, or setting, the guiding question remains: Do public school-based elemen-

---

[1] Zoltan Kodály, *The Selected Writings* (New York: Boosey & Hawkes, 1974) 120.

tary choruses have the capacity to marvel high-stakes audiences? I believe they do. Do they have the ability to sing well and perform quality repertoire with poise and expressiveness? Definitely. Can the general music teacher fulfill the role of children's choir director and provide instruction that helps the students sound like a chorus rather than a bunch of kids singing together? Certainly. Is it enough for the kids to simply participate, or should there be standards for membership, musicianship, and behavior within the ensemble? Can regular kids achieve a heightened level of performance with all of the multiple variables existing in public school settings?

Over time, I've learned that "regular kids" are capable of extraordinary achievements. Bartle wrote, "Everything emanates from the heart, mind, and soul of the teacher."[2] It's up to the educator to structure the learning environment to guide children toward astonishing results.

> A great teacher/conductor must have the philosophy that children can discover and appreciate great art by performing great art....They will never develop a music program that enriches the lives of students, parents, staff, administrators, and members of the community by having the students sing junk.[3]

Based on this premise and belief, further questions emerge:

1. What skills, qualities, and knowledge should the elementary music teacher possess for successful leadership and direction of a school-based chorus?
2. How can instruction within the general music class be designed and adapted to support those techniques specific to teaching a choral ensemble comprised of diverse learners?
3. Who will be in the chorus? How will members be solicited, selected, and maintained?
4. What setting, materials, and staff are needed before rehearsals begin?
5. What body of repertoire should be utilized? Where can it be found and how can it be prepared for instruction with students who might not be familiar reading choral music?

[2] Jean Ashworth Bartle, *Sound Advice: Becoming a Better Children's Choir Director* (New York: Oxford University Press, 2003) 87.
[3] Ibid., 87.

6. What preparatory steps should be taken before re-hearsals occur?
7. Where and when will the chorus perform? For whom?
8. What should chorus members wear? Why is this important?
9. Should field trips, tours, and off-school campus performances take place? How are these organized and executed?
10. Who are the key constituents to consider? What mode of communication will be most effective between the director and his or her constituents?

Why This Book?

While authors have contributed to the wealth and knowledge of choral techniques, conducting strategies, and rehearsal tips, most are written with the secondary choral director in mind. The more prominent texts for children's choir instruction are designed for those working with professional groups (Bartle, Rao) or within the church setting (McRae). Linda Swears published a very useful text on elementary school choruses in 1985, but as many veteran educators can attest, the population of children in our schools differs dramatically from two decades past, inviting strategies that can be adapted to this changing reality.

Inside the Elementary School Chorus is designed with four primary audiences in mind:

1. General music teachers who have a choir within their school setting and are seeking tips to consider for improved instruction;
2. General music teachers who've been asked to begin a choir at their school and are looking for suggestions on how that process might begin effectively;
3. Any music educator who finds an opportunity to establish a non-auditioned children's chorus (church or community setting); and
4. Pre-service/in-service music educators currently enrolled in undergraduate or graduate choral or general music methods.

An added feature of this book is the accompanying DVD, which provides both sight and sound to strategies shared in narrative. Students in the Canyon Creek 5th/6th-grade chorus (2007–2008) of Bothell, Washington, as well as 4th-, 5th-, and 6th-grade students in general music classroom settings (at Canyon Creek) allowed cameras to record lessons, rehearsals, and a performance in support of this text. In truth, these regular kids in a regular K–6 public school—my students (of whom I'm exceptionally proud)—are the real teachers and the real stars.

The DVD is organized into sections that accompany basic foundations of the book:

1. The general music classroom as a venue for vocal instruction
2. Rehearsal strategies for the public school elementary chorus
3. Performances—before, during, and after

Inside the Elementary School Chorus

The book is divided into chapters that combine insights gained from professional literature, observations, and interviews of other children's choir directors, as well as trial and error on my part. The reading is friendly and direct and doesn't assume that every tip will work for every teacher. These are collected ideas that have been read, tested, or evolved from one general music teacher's pursuit to improve the quality of music instruction, specifically in singing and choral pedagogy, for public school students.

The first chapter, "The General Music Teacher as Children's Choir Director," looks at the specific position of the general music teacher as children's choir director of the students in her school. The realities of the job, the time commitment, the clientele, as well as the support of classroom teachers and administrators are all factors to consider before offering choir as an option. The daily schedule of a full-time general music teacher is already packed with extended programs and performances beyond the school day. This chapter considers principles of pedagogy (vocal and other) that correlate with the role of music teacher/choral director.

Once the music teacher has made a commitment to focus on vocal instruction, she needs to know some basics about the child singing voice. Multiple contributors to the professional literature on children's singing agree that singing is a learned behavior. It's the teacher's job to find those strategies necessary to guide students toward a degree of vocal accuracy. The goal of Chapter Two, "The Child Singing Voice," is to help educators become aware of instructional options, knowing full well that students arrive in their classrooms with a wide range of dispositions and attitudes toward singing in general. Specific texts are outlined and suggested for further investigation of this topic.

Since a public school is comprised of diverse learners, how do elementary music teachers solicit members for their chorus? Chapter Three, "Membership in the Non-Select Chorus," centers on the identification, selection, and maintenance of chorus personnel. After all, without a cohort of students (who understand what they are choosing to be a part of), the chorus is limited in every arena. While volunteer, non-auditioned groups work for some chorus directors, a "ya'll come" model didn't work for me. (In fact, the one time I offered an open, no-strings-attached ensemble it resulted in inconsistent attendance, lack of commitment from students and their parents, and a serious wave of apathy from me!) Membership is a crucial entity and must be approached with thought and planning long before the ensemble meets. This chapter includes sample contracts, communiqués, and techniques used to attract and maintain students to ensemble participation.

Selecting what will be used as curricular fodder and support personnel is shared in Chapter Four, "Repertoire, Materials, and Resources." Without quality literature to perform, students become disillusioned. The current supply of superb

choral music for children's voices is abundant. A director does need to establish criteria for what his choir will sing based on membership, time with the group, and a dozen other considerations. Establishing criteria based on one's personnel and clientele (school community) is crucial. Included in this chapter are suggested programming tips and an annotated list of field-tested octavos. There is also an appendix of additional resources the public school choir director might consider.

Once rehearsals begin, organization is key. Setting the stage for effective learning, behavior, and levels of participation is discussed in Chapter Five, "Rehearsal and Management Strategies." While some students may join for social reasons ("I joined because my friends were in chorus"), all must adhere to a code of rehearsal etiquette as dictated and taught by the director. Expectations for what is to be achieved and adhered to during rehearsals must be crystal clear for all involved. (I can't think of anything less pleasurable than spending 90 minutes with a group of 80 ten to twelve year olds who find chorus rehearsal a place to chat among their buddies the whole time!) Chapter Five considers both the music making and conduct of its members and outlines suggestions for the teacher/director to apply for effective rehearsal techniques.

I believe most choruses of merit have one overriding goal: To perform superb choral literature with musicianship and pride, honoring the composer/arranger with best efforts. Performance is the ultimate goal—it is the culminating event for this learning activity. In Chapter Six, "Purposeful Performances," a variety of considerations are discussed that help those culminating events be memorable and pleasurable, and display the level of achievement you and your students have worked so hard for.

Throughout the text, parallel content on the DVD is mentioned, allowing the reader an option to watch an example of the activity described. Viewing the DVD will enhance the reading experience before, during, or after reading the text.

Belief Systems and Bottom Lines

The elementary children's chorus is comprised of students who elect to be a part of an ensemble led by an adult committed to preparing lessons for rehearsals that result in performances that please all constituents involved (students, parents, the community at large, and the director). Sounds simple. I won't kid you—it takes work. Often, very hard work. Then, why do it?

Teachers who elect to begin and sustain a chorus at their schools have articulated that why. They often revisit their "why" each and every year, to keep enthusiasm and commitment alive and well. Philosophical foundations—the "why" of instructional priorities—provide a compass and an underlying drive; one's foundations advise instruction, they reflect perceptions of ourselves and our students, they give us energy and purpose.

Over time, I've come to realize that offering chorus at my school (and previous schools and communities prior to this position) is an extension of why I teach in the first place. I offer chorus so that the students I teach might experience artistic success that helps them live in personal and civil happiness, with the ability to recognize and value those entities and qualities that make life a joyful adventure. I believe this is possible through a rich and varied education, with opportunities for students to describe, respond, create, and perform artistically with resources and materials that involve, instruct, and inspire.

There are many routes to fulfillment, so why do I offer chorus? Bottom line? I love hearing children sing well. It fills me with personal and professional joy. The sound of kids singing with musicianship, pride, and artistry feeds my soul. That's why I do it. It's a win-win situation: If I'm doing my job appropriately, the students gain, as do I.

I'm fortunate to have a setting that supports the formation of a choral ensemble. Surrounding myself with others who believe in the extraordinary capacity of regular kids in a regular school makes the entire process better. As many a veteran music educator will attest, cultivating an atmosphere of extended support is essential.

I would like to offer my sincerest thanks to my colleagues at Canyon Creek and to Bill Bagnall, Principal, for supporting this project. It goes above and beyond their day-to-day support of the overall music program. My thanks also to the Northshore School District for providing support for the production of the DVD.

Hopefully, this text and accompanying DVD will provide the suggestions you're seeking for positive results with your students. Thanks for your interest and enjoy going inside the non-select elementary children's chorus.

Acknowledgments

My sincerest thanks go to the effort, support, patience, affection, and guidance of Kris Kropff and the other wonderful people at The Lorenz Corporation.

Thanks to Kerry MacDonald, Producer, and Bruce Fisher, Videographer, for putting together a DVD that shows the essence of what goes on at Canyon Creek. You were both a blast to work with.

To my colleagues at Canyon Creek and to Bill Bagnall, Principal: I hope you know all of this would not be possible without your support and guidance.

Mary Lynn Lightfoot's cheerleading and enthusiasm for this project sustained me through the writing and recording process. Your inspiration and friendship continue to be a tremendous source of energy and strength to me.

Mark Mayberry, you are an amazing person to work with and your photos aren't bad either! Your big voice of support means so much to all of us. Thank you, on behalf of Canyon Creek Chorus members—past, current, and future.

To members of the 2007–2008 and 2008–2009 Canyon Creek Chorus: A thousand thank yous to all of you (and your parents).

For the multiple ways you've contributed to the chorus, a special thank you to my friend and colleague Yuh-Pey Lin. You are an extraordinary musician and teacher.

My parents: You have shown that love of one's profession makes life all the better. To my mother, Marjorie Kathleen Smith: Nothing replaces your absence in my life. I miss you and love you.

Finally, to my husband, Tom, daughters Katherine and Julie, and Tiger, our cat: You've gone through this book-writing business twice and continued to support me. Now that's real love! A project like this wouldn't happen without your support.

Inside the Elementary School Chorus

The General Music Teacher as Children's Choir Director

We music educators tend to identify ourselves by what we do. It's a curious thing. I rarely hear secondary educators refer to themselves as music teachers; rather, they usually describe their occupation more specifically: "I'm a band director." "I teach orchestra." Secondary choral directors are heard saying, "I'm the choir director at the local high school." In contrast, elementary teachers normally respond, "I teach music," when asked by others what they do. Why is this a significant point? We tend to practice what we perceive as significant to our professional identities.

Normally, elementary music teachers see themselves as generalists rather than specialists. They typically see each child in their school and over time bear witness to their growth and maturity as people and as music makers. Elementary general music teachers engage students in moving, singing, playing instruments, and creating and improvising music. They teach children to listen attentively and responsively. They show musical instruments, and share songs and dances of the world.

Within the elementary music classroom, students grow in confidence, skill, and awareness of themselves as music participants. This is where the seeds of expanded, enhanced, and continued music involvement are planted. During general music lessons, students begin to apply those qualities seen, heard, and experienced by members of music-making communities, like choral ensembles.

According to Gregoryk, the general music classroom provides an environment that leads students toward engagement in choral activities. These include:

- Applying the ability and response to conducting gesture
- Developing a mental concept of good choral tone
- Learning to work with others to produce a blended sound
- Attending to diction and uniformity of vowels
- Singing and listening to a wide range of vocal styles and genres
- Developing music reading skills[1]

These facets of choral music are blended into the myriad of other skills generalists include as the norm in general music. (The reader will recognize many of these skills when viewing the first chapter of the DVD.)

Although general music teachers might employ skills akin to choral experiences, we differ from secondary music instructors in our perceptions, patterns, and progress with students. We refer to our students in classroom groups, not ensembles. We organize lessons based on grade levels and developmental preparedness rather than ensemble repertoire and literature. Different from the secondary conductor, our students come to our general music classes as part of a given routine, not by choice. We are their music teachers first and, if offered within the school setting, their ensemble director a distant second.

The Public School-Based Chorus

The school's general music teacher normally directs choral ensembles offered in an elementary school as an extension of her regular position. There are many reasons why chorus is offered at some schools but not available to students at others. The following reasons for the inclusion or additional of chorus into the fabric of one's school setting were consistently revealed in discussions with several elementary music teacher friends:

- The music educator's own desire and intent to establish a choral ensemble that meets beyond the full-time teaching assignment.
- A school's tradition; that is, a pre-existing group is part of the culture and content of the music teacher's job expectations.
- The community surrounding the school strongly suggests the creation of a choral group (e.g., "The school

---

[1] Joan Gregoryk, "Choral Music Education Begins in the Classroom," *Choral Journal* 46, no. 10 (April 2006): 32.

three miles from here has a chorus for their older students. Why don't we?")
- A specific event (festival, choral invitational, etc.) promotes the addition of a short-term ensemble to meet outside of the general music classroom.
- The general music position is not full-time and in order to achieve that employment level, the teacher may elect to offer chorus during the day for a specific population of students.

Regardless of which factor applies, elementary music teachers who elect to offer a choral ensemble are accepting a shift in their identity. Coordinating and conducting choral activities alters those routines normally executed by the general music specialist. While "good teaching" is the expectation for both, conducting a choral ensemble of public school students calls for knowledge and skills related to the performing art of choral music above and beyond the multifaceted instructional processes applied in general music.

Swears indicated that effective elementary school choral directors exhibit the following skills and qualities:

- An understanding and ability to interpret music notation accurately and expressively
- An understanding of vocal production and techniques
- Has specific knowledge of the qualities and limitations of the child voice
- Conducts with clarity and expressiveness
- Possesses adequate organizational skill for planning and implementing a choral program[2]

Swears continued, indicating that the musical knowledge and skills are most effectively shared with children when the choral director "likes children" and believes the additional time with them is worthwhile and important. Possessing a healthy sense of humor and confidence in one's own musicianship is also a plus. Finally, Swears indicated that effective children's choir directors "exhibit warmth and acceptance" toward students and recognize both the limitations and possibilities of the ensemble.[3]

---

[2] Linda Swears, *Teaching the Elementary School Chorus* (West Nyack, NY: Parker Publishing, 1985) 7.
[3] Ibid.

McRae wrote that directors should "expect the best of children, as it bestows a dignity upon them that other generations have not always done."[4] Expecting the best of students accompanies high expectations for their teachers and directors. Children tend to rise to the standard held before them; it's the teacher/director's job to not shortchange the choral experience by giving it the same status as a "group of kids who get together and sing."

Defining the Public School Children's Chorus

Describing oneself as a children's choir director goes beyond putting large groups of children together for a one-time singing engagement. That reflects the identity of a general music teacher who is preparing for a school assembly or program performance with multiple classrooms involved.

For the purpose of clarification, in this text, the elementary school children's chorus is described as an ensemble of singers who attend consistent and scheduled rehearsals comprised of members who choose to be a part of an ensemble that rehearses music varied in genre. The repertoire selected is carefully chosen by an informed director and is appropriate for the vocal development of young musicians meeting beyond the general music classroom. The chorus, as defined in this text, includes a director who brings vocal and musical skills to the group and selects material that has the capacity to ignite both enjoyment and educational value to her students.

The successful children's choir director within a public school knows how to invite children into a different kind of learning environment—an environment of high-stakes self-management, anticipated vocal involvement, and improved acuity, along with a sense of belonging to and connecting with peers in a unique and positive setting. The children's choir director in an elementary school spends personal and professional time investigating repertoire, selecting venues for performance, communicating with a wide array of constituents, structuring rehearsals, and promoting the ensemble as an artistic extension of the overall music program in her school.

In addition, the leader of an elementary school chorus seeks to provide an environment that is both enriching and

---

[4] Shirley W. McRae, *Directing the Children's Choir: A Comprehensive Resource* (New York: Schirmer Books, 1991) 11.

socially engaging for the students. She understands that members of the chorus are also members of her general music class and should not receive a replay or exact duplication of what occurred in music class that day. She implements lesson plans and rehearsal strategies that are unique for the choral setting.

As the chart on page 9 illustrates, there are several key factors related to what a choral director does in order to facilitate an ensemble experience of honorable merit. From the chart, one gleans that the general-music-teacher-turned-children's-choir-director can only do what she knows how to do. At a minimum, the teacher should know how to integrate educational frameworks into the choral arena and she should be able to glance at song material (both public domain and published) and quickly assess its educational and artistic value.

The ability to effectively and consistently communicate with all constituents is critical. And having a clear and varied strategy for notifying parents of events and dates is just as important as being able to communicate a musical idea. Beyond all of the paperwork and musical analysis, establishing and maintaining some system of behavior and musicianship is key to success. The best conducting skills in the world will not mean a thing if the classroom or rehearsal is a place where chaos reigns!

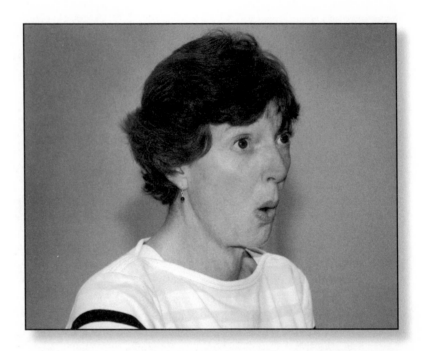

The primary elements of the successful public school children's choir director include the ability to help her students produce a healthy singing voice. This is accomplished through one's ability to model in such a manner that children can listen and learn. Perhaps most significant and vital is the teacher's ability to inform chorus members of rehearsal etiquette and procedures.

The children's choir director hones skills that provide her choristers with effective sequential instruction, quality repertoire that fits the group, and a genuine interest in establishing a musical community that has meaning and purpose to everyone involved. It is so much more than combining classrooms to sing a song!

Good Public School Children's Choirs Grow Out of Singing Classrooms

Quality children's choirs at the public school level grow out of classrooms that sing. Good singing classrooms grow out of a teacher's ability to provide motivating vocal experiences for all students. In order for quality singing experiences to occur on a consistent basis, a culture of singing must be created within the music classroom. The overriding culture and community established within the general music classroom comes from the teacher's day-to-day encounters with students and the rapport, truth, faith, respect, and relationship developed with them.

In order to establish a chorus of merit, a teacher…

Develops the child's singing voice so that it can produce a healthy, in-tune, and musical tone

Identifies chorus members by establishing criteria for membership based on what the student demonstrates

Selects repertoire that fits the voices, the age, rehearsal schedule, and support personnel available

Demonstrates in body and voice, what a singer looks like, sounds like, rehearses like (modeling is key)

Sequences instruction so that not only will the chorus sound good, but musicianship will grow

What a teacher does depends on what the teacher knows how to do

Interpret and implement standards and benchmarks

Analyze music and recognize instructional strategies

Communicate with students, staff, parents, community

Establish and maintain expectations for behavior and musicianship

Good teachers understand that a positive learning environment fuels learning to new levels: Ordinary activities become enhanced and more enjoyable when they become part of the fabric and nature of what is considered to be normal. Although singing is part of the fabric of a complete elementary music education, establishing a community of quality singers requires tremendous commitment and consistency on the part of the teacher throughout the tenure of a child's general music involvement.

New students to the school may find it difficult at first to embrace the idea of quality singing (if coming from a different kind of elementary school culture); some may even challenge the practice of singing well. But most socially healthy students will quickly become accustomed to the culture and rituals of the school, particularly those traits that the majority of the students perceive as "just what we do here."

Developing a singing culture within the general music classroom takes time, consistent communication, and the development of trust with the adults in charge. Swears wrote:

> Beyond having specific skills and knowledge, there are certain personal qualities that enable one to work effectively with children. Children will not automatically respond to good musicianship on the teacher's part. There must be an attitude of caring that permeates the student-teacher relationship.[5]

Since singing is the heart and soul of music education (which is why it hurts so much when done poorly), elementary generalists must develop techniques to engage students in singing activities that build confidence, ability, and achievement. Learning to sing is natural for some students, but others will advance when taught by an informed, patient, caring music educator who believes all children have the capacity to use their voices in musical ways. An attitude of caring must be blended with a strong sense of what is developmentally acceptable and what is not at each stage apparent in an elementary level.

How does that occur? What strategies lead to the creation of a singing culture inside the K–6 general music classroom? Why is it a vital component of an outstanding public school children's choir?

---

[5] Swears, 7.

Creating a Singing Culture Within the General Music Classroom: Cultivating a Learning Environment

Public schools in most geographical areas tend to have a diverse population of students. Within this diverse population one finds students with variable degrees of comfort and confidence levels in singing. While some wholeheartedly and enthusiastically participate in large- and small-group singing, others are timid and reserved. Some express opposition and will either not sing or will make singing a big joke, resulting in sounds that oppose any musical attributes desired.

Prior to discussing strategies specific to singing, it would be negligent to not interject comments regarding the broader learning environment. Within the music classroom or rehearsal venue, nothing can be accomplished if chaos ensues. Beyond the musical skills required of the generalist and the choir director, a system of organization that promotes learning must be established and promoted.

Classrooms that encourage civil obedience and citizenship accountability will see improved results. A system that promotes personal responsibility and respect for people and processes does spurn a positive learning environment. Unfortunately, there is not an exact time frame to determine how long this effort will take. It must be taught, reinforced, and believed in. It is not simple; however, in our current 21st-century public school settings, it is necessary.[6]

When students are given clear and concise communication, modeling, practice, and feedback of what learning looks like and sounds like in a classroom, they are likely to adhere to the expectation (if delivered by a teacher who has established a level of rapport and trust). How long does it take to turn a non-singing school culture into a singing one? As long as it takes! Consistency of expectations—day after day, week after week, month after month, year after year—will eventually have a positive effect.

I do not promote a sterile classroom or rehearsal scenario where the teacher reigns supreme. I do, however, promote an environment that emphasizes personal and material safety; where behavioral and academic achievement is the expectation for all. Students function more freely and are less fearful of risk if they have faith in their teachers and know peers adhere to

---

[6] Randy Sprick, et al. *The Safe and Civil Schools Series: Proactive, Positive, and Instructional Discipline* (Eugene, OR: Safe and Civil Schools, 2005, CD-ROM).

the same standard of behavior. This is particularly vital when engaging a diverse group of students in singing activities.

"Singing is a phenomenon for all ages, times, and cultures, but it begins and is nurtured in childhood."[7] The general music teacher has the unique capacity to influence the singing confidence and competence of her students at a crucial time in their childhood. By investing consistent instruction and encouragement, positive results can be established from the beginning of a child's tenure in the music classroom.

Since I teach in an elementary school with grades K–6, students begin their general music classes at the age of 5 and, if the family remains in the neighborhood, continue attending general music classes through age 12. What an opportunity! If I do my job well, students grow up learning specific skills and physical habits that will strengthen singing activities and over-all musicianship. Most elementary general music teachers will agree that, in most cases, younger children tend to embrace singing more readily and confidently than older.

Regardless of grade level, one of my primary goals for all students is to establish and maintain a desire to fully engage and participate in their learning, whether the musical activity is singing, moving, listening, playing instruments, or a combination of all. All are appealing ways to facilitate understanding and can be enjoyable and motivating when incorporated in developmentally appropriate ways. General music teachers understand this and strive to provide multiple avenues for acquiring musical understanding.

In the kindergarten and primary grades, students normally enjoy a wide range of activities and will usually not hesitate to join in. Given the school's "singing culture," general music lessons for younger children begin with song games, echo songs, vocal exploration, call and response, folk songs, songs that relate to events or holidays, invented songs, rounds, partner songs, etc. Songs are selected that invite participation and contribute to the students' increasing skills.

Beyond providing a varied and meaningful repertoire of songs, there are a few very simple goals I have for younger students in their vocal instruction. Instructional strategies accompany each of these goals; however, my primary intent is to establish a learning environment where singing is natural, enjoyable, and something students look forward to participating in. Other basic goals for grades K–3 follow.

---

[7] Patricia Shehan Campbell and Carol Scott-Kassner, *Music in Childhood: From Preschool through the Elementary Grades* (New York: Schirmer Books, 1995) 127.

Kindergarten students (ages five and six)
- Discern and demonstrate the differences between the singing voice and other voices (speaking, yelling, whispering, etc.)
- Keep jaw, face, and head clear of hands while singing

First grade (ages six and seven)
- Reinforce skills from kindergarten
- Begin to recognize (aurally and visually) and physically show pitch and rhythmic changes (ascending/descending, long/short, etc.)
- Begin to hear and interpret the words "use your best singing voice" and react by adjusting posture (dropping hands, etc.)

Second grade (ages seven and eight)
- By habit, consistently resist touching the face, jaw, and hair while singing
- Recognize ascending, descending, static pitches visually and aurally (isolated samples) and within a melody
- Show an understanding of singing posture when directed to do so
- Expanded accuracy in pitch and tonal matching within an octave (C to c')
- Recognize when two pitches are the same and when they are different (aurally)

Third grade (ages eight and nine)
- Consistently demonstrate singing posture when given a prompt to do so
- Follow melodies with accuracy, especially those with text below the notes
- Recognize melodic patterns, identifying what is seen with increased musical vocabulary
- Increase confidence and accuracy in singing alone or in parts (rounds, partner songs, etc.)
- Identify and implement those personal habits that are necessary for using "best singing voice"
- Follow a conductor as well as imitate the role of the conductor in classroom singing

At the intermediate grades, insecure students, or those concerned about ridicule or boredom, will choose to opt out of participating in activities that might cause personal embarrassment or distress. When cultivating a singing culture, particularly with 4th grade (ages nine and 10) and higher, teachers must carefully weigh the balance between high standards and expectations and student comfort. The educator must clearly communicate the desired standards and consistently remind students of them. At the same time, she must adhere to some level of empathetic understanding; some students may need time to grow comfortable with their voices. If presented with respect and clear of embarrassment and ridicule, qualities of resilience and risk-taking will emerge in students who might otherwise not engage in singing activities positively.

Any learned behavior, like quality singing, comes from knowing what to do, how to do it, and why doing it brings about positive results. If begun at the earliest stages of a child's tenure in the school and reinforced, the skills are practiced and applied until they become habits of mind and body. Successful general music classrooms promote those "habits of mind" that can be tremendous assets in a performing ensemble, above and beyond singing well. These habits include:

- Developing self-discipline and self-monitoring skills
- Experiencing and inspiring confidence in self and others
- Increasing one's willingness to stretch his comfort zone and be challenged
- Developing tools and techniques for functioning within a group
- Finding honor in positive results and attitudes

While it would be nice to believe all students will pursue the highest level of these habits, in some of our public schools that's simply unrealistic; it avoids the fact that there are some kids so very troubled that positive movement forward is a daunting task. This doesn't excuse educators from establishing classrooms and ensembles that give students the opportunity to experience solid instruction in a respectful environment of learning. If students have issues impairing healthy and productive learning, that's the *most* critical time to implement a culture of civility and citizenship.

Barbara Colorose is quoted as stating:

> If kids come to us (educators/teachers/directors) from
> strong, healthy, functioning families, it makes our job
> easier. If they do not come to us from strong, healthy,
> functioning families, it makes our job more important.[8]

Teachers, state what you want to hear in your students'
singing activities. Describe and model what you want to see
them do when singing occurs. Provide a variety of song material that is appropriately voiced and set to texts that give opportunity for thought or laughter or interest or curiosity.

Consistently encourage singing habits that help voices
improve. Identify those who might need assistance. Remind
students what the expectations are for the basics of singing:
posture, breath support, expressive faces, etc. Develop instructional approaches that emphasize those vocal habits that
help make singing a pleasurable experience.

Students at my school will often hear statements that remind them of the singing expectation for our classroom community. For example, "When kindergarteners and 1st graders
sing at Canyon Creek, they keep their faces clear for all to see."
Others include, "At Canyon Creek, 4th graders know to keep
their hands and arms down while singing," and "At Canyon

---

[8] Erin Gruwell, editor, *The Gigantic Book of Teacher's Wisdom* (New
York: Skyhorse Publishing, 2007).

Creek, 6th graders do sing and set the bar high for using solid singing habits." Another heard in many classrooms: "When people watch Canyon Creek students sing, they see and hear people who know what they're doing!" These statements help build the idea that singing well is just part of what Canyon Creek students do.

When substitute teachers or observers come to Canyon Creek, they are often surprised with the participation level in classroom-singing experiences, particularly with the older students. What they don't know is the amount of time, energy, and commitment it has taken to create that culture! Each and every fall, classroom singing expectations are taught—a review for some and new for others. Each year, I remind returning students what the expectations are and ask new students to glance around the room to examine, for themselves, the standard for classroom singing. Repeating this process year after year would get tiring if the results weren't so very much worth it!

So, if students are singing in the general music classroom with reasonable success, why offer a choral ensemble? Beyond the singing classroom, I believe the availability of a choir keeps those who enjoy singing, and do so beautifully and artistically, engaged and challenged. At the same time, it can't help but improve the singing voices of all participants, regardless of vocal status. Each has an opportunity to excel as singers—to go above and beyond the classroom scene.

Professionally, my goal for the classroom and the choral ensemble has been defined, refined, and trimmed to include more non-musical direction than musical. I strive to create an atmosphere where learning is possible. I strive to help each class that walks in my room, particularly those at the intermediate level, know that I'm paying attention to their individual response, their level of participation, and the comfort (or lack thereof) demonstrated while singing or engaging in other music-making endeavors. I strive to shift the age-old paradigm from "what will *I* teach" to "what will *they* learn." This philosophical application keeps my eyes and ears focused on what I see and what I hear. Finally, each successive year reminds me to not quit on any student.

In order to establish a 5th- and 6th-grade children's chorus at my school, membership grows from students' perceptions of singing well as a worthwhile thing to do. If vocal instruction is not taught within the general music classroom, students have no idea how great they can sound when simple strategies are placed in action. The instruction must be suitable for all students—those who love to sing as well as those who shy away or refuse to invest (at first).

Singing Expectations for the Classroom

Within the music classroom, singing strategies are employed and directed to the whole class. Expectations are communicated, modeled, and practiced in hopes they will become habits. Students actively participate; they display skills, understanding, and an emerging disposition toward singing. The general music teacher uses her intuition, her management systems, and her knowledge of teaching singing to guide students toward an attitude and ability that results in quality vocal experiences.

Within my 3rd through 6th-grade general music classrooms, I ask for the following basic skills to be displayed by all students. (Bits and pieces of the skills described below can be viewed in the first section of the accompanying DVD, as demonstrated by 4th-, 5th-, and 6th-grade students.)

1. Posture is tall and proud. Weight is balanced on both feet; hands and arms are down to the side. Shoulders are relaxed. Thigh muscles are strong but not stiff.
2. Breath is active and focused. Support for sound is directed from the diaphragm. The exhalation of air is paced so that a student notices the sustaining sense of controlled breath.
3. Pitch matching occurs teacher to student, student to teacher. An "oo" vowel is used, person to person, beginning with two descending pitches. If the pitch is not matched, the teacher model is changed to more closely relate to that pitch heard from the student.
4. Vowels are shaped and attention to the work and investment of facial muscles is discussed. Diction, articulation, and supporting the text of a song are reinforced.
5. Emphasis on expanded range, registration, and phonation occur. Sirens from the highest head tone down become normal and are described as effective ways to stretch the vocal mechanism. Head tone is described as projecting a "unicorn horn from the forehead and placing the voice out the tip of the horn." The chest voice is referred to as a heavier sound and appropriate when the range of pitches is more comfortably sung in

that heavier range, or the genre of the song calls for that particular registration.

6. Increased vocabulary occurs alongside increased music-reading skills. "Musician speak" is the norm, with vocal and musical tenets described in terms common to those who participate in music. Reading skills progress from the need to utilize the interpretation and application of music symbols.

7. Active participation is expected and considered the norm for all students. Attention is given to the group's investment and involvement as well as attention to the individual.

8. Acceptance and tolerance is demonstrated when learning songs, especially those with non-English texts.

These strategies are practiced and employed with entire classes. In my experience, they provide the backbone for establishing a singing classroom. I understand that singing together is a social occurrence and can occur without a series of instructional steps, but if I truly want students to improve as singers, basic foundations need to be employed.

Within each classroom, individuals have their own unique needs for enhanced singing experiences. "Unique" individuals sometimes require "unique instruction." Trollinger noted, "Vocal development is highly individual and not every tactic will work for every child."[9] Experience proves her completely correct on this point.

The Tales of the Six

One of the best ways to share strategies for working with individual, diverse learners and voices in the general music classroom is to tell stories. I call these stories the tales of the "six." These six names represent real students in my professional career and offer insight as to how their particular vocal acuity was addressed. In all cases, the instructional techniques used were a result of trial and error, consequential change, or unforeseen events that altered the playing field. These individuals range from Renee, who represents a 6th-grade girl with excellent vocal skills, to Carl, a 6th-grade boy who defiantly refused to open his mouth to sing.

In most cases, the strategies described here seemed to help move the student along a progressive trail. In some cases, the strategies merely reinforced the strength of the student's abilities in singing. In others, it helped the classroom environment by convincing the individual to nix the saboteur attitude when it involved singing. Three of the six elected to participate in chorus, although their vocal skill and original disposition for singing varied dramatically.

These tales represent attempts to, first and foremost, create a singing culture in the classroom where students would be held accountable for improved singing skills. Secondly, the students described (with invented names) were in 5th or 6th grade at the time and thus eligible to participate in chorus. Some of the strategies used were designed to help the student feel bolstered and supported in his or her contribution to the choral ensemble. (Some of the strategies described in these tales can be viewed in the first chapter of the DVD. Since these individuals come from varying periods of time, the overt strategies might look and sound familiar; however, none of the six are specifically seen or heard by viewers.)

---

[9] Valerie Trollinger, "Pediatric Vocal Development and Voice Science: Implications for Teaching Singing," *General Music Today* 20, no. 3 (spring 2007): 23.

No doubt some of the student descriptions will strike a familiar chord with many elementary general music teachers, as most experienced public school music educators have taught kids who resemble Renee and have met with the initial frustration that comes with teaching someone like Carl.

The Tale of Renee

Renee is the oldest of three children. She attended the same school and was a student in my music classes from kindergarten to 6th grade. She exuded confidence in all she did, academically, socially, and in her friendships with others. Vocally, she always matched pitch, raised her hand to vocally model, and chose to participate in choir both years it was available to her (5th and 6th grade). For Renee, singing was an activity she loved. Her confidence was evident in the level of participation shown in class and in chorus (volunteering to be first, volunteering to lead warm-ups, volunteering to sing solos, etc.).

Listening to Renee sing, one could immediately surmise her enthusiasm for singing could be extended to challenges beyond simple vocal experiences. Renee was ready to experience a wider range of repertoire, with challenging vocal blends, harmonic consonance, and dissonance. She could be called upon to carry a part independently. Renee was ready to learn the traits necessary to be a vocal leader, perhaps in the role of a student director.

Strategies

1. Teach Renee basic conducting techniques and invite her to utilize these skills in class and chorus rehearsal.
2. Invite Renee to vocally model.
3. Engage Renee, when appropriate, as a leader of sectionals in chorus.
4. Provide Renee and her family information about professional auditioned groups available for superb singers.
5. Encourage Renee to pursue music lessons beyond the school day (piano, etc.).

Renee continued to be very active in music. She played in the school orchestra and sang in chorus. During our last communiqué, I learned she was thoroughly enjoying piano lessons as well.

The Tale of Ken

Ken was a big, friendly 5th grader when he first arrived at our school, having transferred from another state. The first time we sang in class after his arrival, I immediately heard an amazing tone coming from this young man. I mentioned what a great voice he had, privately at first (not knowing how he'd receive this compliment), and he smiled and replied with a hearty thank you. It was obvious he was comfortable with his voice as well as his "manliness" and (thankfully) had a great musical start in his previous elementary school.

I really liked this kid! He had an easy-going personality, and didn't hesitate to participate in all music activities.

Singing was definitely his strongest musical skill. He had tremendous vocal confidence, and often stood right in front of the piano where I could hear him loud and clear. (I think he really enjoyed the big smile appearing on my face when I'd hear him sing.)

I fully expected him to sign up for chorus. He didn't. I waited a while then approached him, recapping what a strong singer he was and how much he would contribute to (and learn from) being in the group. He said, "I just really don't want to join the group, but thanks for asking. I have football practice in the afternoon anyway." What a disappointment!

Ken and his fully resonant head tone became my "go to guy" for demonstration in class. As his voice was nearing a change, the brilliance of that head tone was stunning. Since chorus was something he really didn't want to do, my greatest worry was that he would stop singing all together, since music class is optional in the junior high.

Strategies

1. Include information about the changing male voice so that Ken (and others like him) could understand what might occur and to continue to find ways to keep the singing voice engaged.
2. Provide opportunities for Ken to be chorally challenged in the music classroom, by selecting repertoire that celebrated that brilliant head tone of his.
3. Have Ken lead sections when singing rounds and/or partner songs.

By the way, Ken did join chorus the following year.

The Tale of Kathy

Kathy didn't hesitate to sing in class and wouldn't resist the quick echo sessions included as part of warm-up routines. She could easily shape her mouth to have a picture perfect "oo" or "ah." When singing occurred in class, she'd respond to instructional ideas, both those directed towards her and those directed towards others. Kathy was, in most respects, a fine singer. She was not, however, a leader. Her personality was pleasant, but she liked being relatively unnoticed. To be singled out and asked to show a specific skill was something she was never comfortable with. Her overall musical abilities were strong enough to be a leader, but the discomfort it caused her wasn't worth losing her faith and trust.

In quick, private comments, I'd let her know how terrific she looked and sounded while singing. She'd not respond affirmatively, but would continue each week to engage and participate full throttle. While I wanted to say, "Hey everyone! Check out Kathy! Now that's how it's to be done!," it would have caused tremendous averse results. For Kathy, quiet acknowledgement of what she did right and not calling on her to model seemed to work best.

Strategies

1. Listen to Kathy's voice while group singing occurs (walking around room to listen) and acknowledge the positive attributes of her voice privately.
2. Encourage Kathy's participation in choir, placing her carefully between more dominant personalities (knowing she felt more comfortable in a follower role).
3. Encourage Kathy to pursue participation in instrumental ensembles (strings or band), since diverting her eyes toward a music stand seems more comforting than direct eye-contact with the director or audience.

Kathy never joined chorus; however, she did become a very fine violinist and continues to play in the school orchestra.

The Tale of David

David came from a family where athletics ruled. He was a superb runner, pitcher, and quarterback. He was well coordinated, strong, and confident in his physical/athletic abilities. When it came to any kind of involvement with singing, his immediate reaction (as a little boy) was "this is sissy stuff." My task and challenge was to not get angry about this attitude! Obviously, this was something he'd gleaned elsewhere and he merely manifested that perception.

Each and every year, David needed to be reminded that singing was part of the whole music education package, like it or not. Fortunately, he remained at my school the entire tenure of his elementary years. We established an understanding—I would hold him accountable for doing his best and he would not sabotage quality singing.

Strategies

1. Attend a game or event where David would recognize my support of his skills as athlete, thus altering his image of me as the enemy. (David clearly had issues of image. He feared his masculinity would be called into question if he showed any pleasure in singing. I wanted to be sure he knew I knew he was a tremendous athlete and admired that in him.)
2. Use phrases that were part of David's world: "be strong," "use your muscles," "suck it up, people, let's go!" These seemed to inspire him to take one more step toward healthy participation.
3. Place David by two other athletic (boy) singers (like Ken). If I couldn't help with the masculinity issue he was plagued with, these fellows certainly could (and did!).
4. Emphasize the need to display posture, breath support, and intent to do one's best. (Fortunately, David knew when he was out of tune and made attempts to implement techniques to stretch his singing range.)

David joined chorus during the last semester of his 6th-grade year. He was a very committed and helpful member.

The Tale of Alice

I came to believe something had occurred in Alice's life that caused her to be exceptionally withdrawn, timid, afraid, and inhibited. It worried me, and conversations with her classroom teacher indicated she shared the same concerns. Alice was afraid of being singled out, for either positive or negative reasons. Her inability to invest was most obvious when singing activities ensued. It was almost painful to watch. Alice's posture visibly changed when I came near, as if I might say something that would draw attention to her. She would look down and draw down her shoulders, as if anticipating some kind of blow to occur.

Alice came to my school in November, after the year had begun. She missed all the routines and traditions that normally occur in the early days of school, particularly those exercises that lead to a classroom singing climate.

Strategies

1. Welcome Alice to the school privately (when walking by her in the hall or out on the playground).
2. Notice the peers Alice seems to attach to; in group singing, be sure she is with that person/those people.
3. Encourage Alice's class to feel great about their progress in singing and in working together to support each other, in hopes that she will feel bolstered by that support.
4. Watch Alice sing when she doesn't notice she's being observed.
5. Remind myself that Alice's spirit and self-perception are far more important than assessing her individual abilities in singing.

Alice has yet to pursue membership in any musical ensemble.

The Tale of Carl

Carl arrived in February of his 6th-grade year, having been in a middle school prior to arriving. By the end of the first day, conversations occurred amongst the many adults he would impact. He was one angry young man. We learned his life outside of school was as dismal as it could be—drug-addicted mom, no dad in the picture, and multiple moves in his short 11 years. He had developed little consistency or trust in anyone.

A big guy with strength and an intimidating glance, his classmates learned it was best to not cross him. Regardless of setting, Carl was not inclined to get along with anyone or anything. In music, PE, library, and the classroom, his peers seemed helpless in their attempts to befriend him. A few fellows seemed to admire his rebellious attitude, but swift calls home from school personnel stifled attempts from those student to reenact his deeds.

Having been warned about Carl, it was going to be a challenge to embrace some empathy for this fellow. I'd already developed an opinion of him that was not favorable. The last thing this guy wanted to do was invest in anything social, like singing as a group. The first day he came to music class, he mocked my enthusiasm by screwing up his face and imitating the comments I said to the class. Everything was "stupid" to him—his classmates, this "lame school," learning in general, life in general. Having any expectations that this fellow would drop the attitude and embrace singing as a positive contribution to his life was *totally* unrealistic.

Strategies

1. Obtain as much information as possible regarding Carl. Of particular importance was his history with classroom climate and basic safety.
2. Continue to keep the classroom—especially those in it—safe. If he mocked and ridiculed me, I could take it and would deal with it. But, to do that to others would not be tolerated.
3. Establish a plan that was agreed upon and supported by Carl's classroom teacher and the principal, so that any removal from the class (for safety or bullying issues) was consistently supported and followed a very specific rule of protocol.
4. Remain consistent in what would, should, and could occur in the music classroom. As long as Carl was not sabotaging activities, he was successful. His personal involvement and investment was not the measure of success.
5. Try to keep emotional reaction in perspective. This guy was a victim of unfortunate circumstances. He did not need another adult perceiving him as nothing but trouble.

Carl moved in May, just a few months after arriving. While our school sighed a bit with relief, we had made progress with him, especially his classroom teacher—the first adult male role model Carl had connected with. I still wonder about Carl and am saddened by his tragic circumstances.

As veteran educators will attest, students experience learning through multiple systems. We cannot assume the same instructional strategy will work child to child. According to

Givens, the most powerful learning systems are emotional and social.[10] In the cases of Renee, Ken, Kathy, David, Alice, and Carl, my job as their music teacher was to measure the receptivity and comfort of each before assuming they could, or would, accept instruction. Their ability to open up and be receptive to trust and faith in me/their classmates, plus their identification with peers and cultural norms, drove the strategies employed.

Attention to the personal, developmental, physical, and academic priorities of each and every student is basic to the public school setting. It requires dialogue among the adults in the school building as well as a shared philosophy regarding the child's school experience. With the support of one's colleagues and administrator, music teachers have an opportunity to develop a classroom that accepts the multiple ranges of abilities and acceptance.

In his text, *Music Teaching Style: Moving Beyond Tradition*, Alan Gumm reminded us:

> Students are difficult to motivate in the learning environment if their basic human needs are unmet. Learning is difficult to motivate if the need for love or affection and esteem needs of achievement, independence, and respect go unmet. [Teachers] must come to care for students and know whether their most basic needs are met before the focus is on motivating learning.[11]

Regardless of pre-existing conditions, elementary music teachers have the right and the opportunity to design the kind of classroom experiences that helps learning occur. When students know their teachers care about them as people, resistance to learning diminishes and students begin to accept the vision their music teacher has for their success.

The general music teacher who decides to invest the time, knowledge, energy, and commitment to serve as her school's choir director will be greeted by students with varying singing

---

[10] Barbara K. Given, *Teaching to the Brain's Natural Learning Systems* (Alexandria, VA: Association for Supervision & Curriculum Development, 2002).

[11] Alan Gumm, *Music Teaching Style: Moving Beyond Tradition* (Galesville, MD: Meredith Music Publications, 2003) 138.

abilities and attitudes. While the goal may be to sing quality repertoire in front of diverse and high-stakes audience, the educator must remember that the choral group is made up of individuals who require attention, care, support, and instructional savvy.

I truly believe that ordinary public school children are capable of extraordinary achievements. They have the opportunity to excel when coupled with an educator who combines high expectations with a heart for each and every soul. The choral ensemble can be an excellent organization for enhanced experiences, both musical and social. The general music teacher as children's choir director has an opportunity to watch and listen and marvel at the performance standards made accessible through direct instruction in their classrooms. How rewarding that can be!

The Child
Singing Voice

With or without an organized choral ensemble, the elementary music teacher should have a fundamental understanding of the child singing voice. After all, singing is usually one of the consistent core skills utilized throughout a child's elementary music experience, regardless of the teacher's chosen methodology. The informed music educator should have a general sense of how to emphasize those entities that make singing healthful, successful, and musical.

Stafford wrote:

> The greatest service a music teacher can provide for the young singer is a distinct knowledge of basic vocal principles. If there is a lack of understanding in basic principles, there is little hope of achieving vocal development in all children.[1]

Most music educators learn techniques for vocal involvement within their teacher-preparation program. For those reading this text without that background, the vocal principles Stafford mentioned include emphasis and instruction in:

- Appropriate singing posture
- Utilization of effective breath support
- Accuracy in matching and maintaining pitch
- Placement of tone and vocal registration

[1] Douglas Stafford, "Perceptions of Competencies and Preparation Needed for Guiding Young Singers in Elementary School Music Classes," (DMA diss., The Florida State University, 1987) 47.

- Formation of the mouth and face for vowels and clarity of diction
- Musical awareness of phrase and musical nuance

Singing is an activity that can be assessed through observation of an entire class (as compared to a listening exercise, for instance) as well as listening to each child independently. The inclusion of appropriate posture, the formation of the mouth, and expression in the face, etc., are overt, participation-based activities that allow teachers to use a quick glance to evaluate the level of its application in the general music classroom or choral ensemble.

While teaching the principles of singing will improve the vocal skills of students, progress will be a struggle without an atmosphere of trust, faith, encouragement, and safety. Bartle wrote, "The teacher's need to develop a warm and encouraging manner cannot be emphasized enough."[2] In order for all students to improve, the teacher must have "indefatigable optimism" that singing will not only improve with instruction, but a commitment that it is a professional responsibility to provide both the know-how and passion to guide students toward success.[3]

Goetze noted, "Singing in tune and with a healthy vocal production is possible for nearly all children, but for some this will happen only by the careful guidance of a music teacher."[4] Trollinger emphasized that the child's vocal anatomy is not like that of an adult's, and that an informed music educator should engage children in singing activities that are physiologically within their reach. "Vocal muscles remain largely underdeveloped until the onset of puberty and are prone to problems if made to work too hard in singing."[5]

As a beginning teacher, I knew how to apply skills that helped *my* singing voice work, but was not predisposed to consider implementing basic principles when teaching *children* to sing. I naïvely assumed that kids could either sing in tune or that they couldn't. I didn't understand that singing was a teachable skill and that sequential, informed instruction could resolve one's pitch accuracy issues in all but extreme cas-

---

[2] Bartle, *Sound Advice*, 15.
[3] Ibid.
[4] Douglas Beam, "Respecting the Voice: Four Music Teachers Discuss the Challenges of Teaching Children to Sing," *The Orff Echo* 15 (summer 2008).
[5] Trollinger, 20.

es. I probably selected song material and repertoire that might have conflicted with the children's ranges and their physiological capabilities. In truth, song resources were selected based on two criteria: I knew the songs previously and they were readily available.

Through years of experience, I've learned that teaching children to sing accurately, successfully, and confidently goes beyond the simple knowledge and transmission of the "basics" of singing. In addition, it goes beyond an expanded repertoire and resource of song material. Experience has taught me that the effective public school music teacher must have the ability to intuitively gauge the comfort and confidence level of his students and proceed with that framework in mind. Every public school elementary music teacher knows that one can possess multiple instructional ideas, but unless they are aligned with an individual's receptivity in mind, some students might not achieve the success they could otherwise.

As students age (particularly in upper elementary grades), they tend to become self-conscious and align their overt behaviors with what is considered acceptable among their peers. I have yet to talk with an elementary general music teacher who has not encountered a 4th, 5th, or 6th grader who is resistant to singing in a public setting such as a music classroom. The experience of facing a student who will not sing is startling at first and, for most music educators, can easily result in frustration.

A student's outward behavior toward singing, both positive and negative, comes from his self-confidence, self-awareness, acceptance of expectations, and perceptions of vocal experiences in general. Janice Smith offered a variety of possible reasons for a student's hesitancy, or outright defiance, toward singing:

- Lack of experience
- Lack of confidence
- Auditory processing difficulties
- Hearing impairments
- Physical problems limiting ability to adjust[6]

Students who do engage in singing, but have trouble matching pitch may need intervention to improve. Bartle specifically

---

[6] Janice Smith, "Every Child a Singer: Techniques for Assisting Developing Singers," *Music Educators Journal* 93, no. 2 (November 2006) 29.

addressed a student's inability (or resistance) to work toward matching pitch and suggested the following possible issues:

- Inexperience; lack of exposure
- Psychological reasons: shyness, lack of confidence, not encouraged to sing
- Immaturity or a lack of readiness
- Poor models (if the student has heard only howling rock singers using hoarse, chest voice, they might believe this to be real singing)
- Underdeveloped auditory memory (they can't concentrate or focus aurally)
- Lack of motivation and interest
- Cultural differences
- Coordination issues (for instance, tone matching is impaired if the child hasn't sung enough to experience the sensation of aligning the breath and production of sound to reproduce what is heard accurately)
- Physiological reasons: some children have impaired vocal cords (nodes or nodules)[7]

Phillips noted, "Young children love to sing. It is only as they become older that they become self-conscious and learn that they do not know how to sing. Once they learn they can be taught, their attitudes (often) change."[8] A change in attitude can most certainly occur, and will for many.

For others, especially those who have experienced a number of failures in their lives, fragility is paramount. Developing a joy for singing can easily fall within the bounds of other skills they've attempted in their short lives. Sadly, they've found it easier to retreat, indicating, "I can't do it, I don't want to do it, no one can make me do it."

As a maturing teacher, this attitude continually saddens me. However, I've learned to not take it personally and to insist that quality singing be heard. If a student will not make attempts to improve vocally, they cannot and will not destroy the sounds others make. In addition, they cannot ridicule or bully those who elect to take the steps needed to sing well. I am the person who can create a place where an uncertain or resistant singer can feel safe and encouraged to try. I can pro-

---

[7] Jean Ashworth Bartle, *Lifeline For Children's Choir Directors* (Toronto: Gordon V. Thompson Publishing Corporation, 1988) 13.
[8] Kenneth H. Phillips, *Teaching Kids to Sing*. (New York: Schirmer Books, 1996) 36.

vide the time, space, and individualized information to help a student move forward. All the vocal know-how in the world won't change a student's attitude or inclination to try and learn if he senses the teacher doesn't believe it's worth the time or effort. He will also remain hesitant if the peer group looks upon singing with a negative point of view.

As mentioned in Chapter 1, creating a singing culture within the school community, combined with instructional steps for improved singing, creates a healthy environment for vocally inexperienced students to gain confidence and begin enjoying the benefits of musical engagement with their voices.

Basics and Beyond: The Phillips Curriculum

One of the most complete treatises on the child singing voice is *Teaching Kids to Sing,* by Dr. Kenneth Phillips. It is, by far, the most comprehensive book on teaching students to sing, presenting substantial pragmatic information and strategies for instructing children to sing in tune. In the sixth chapter, Dr. Phillips outlines a vocal-technique curriculum. Each of Phillips's curricular goals is incorporated into 90 exercises described and disseminated within and throughout a 1st- through 12th-grade continuum. In addition, rubrics are provided to measure the success of instruction, divided into grades 1–6, 7–12, and private lesson or audition purposes. (Key elements are summarized here, but I highly recommend a complete reading of the text.)

At the heart of the curriculum is the premise that children and adolescents can be taught to sing and have the right to learn to sing. Phillips admits the skill is complex, requiring "three major forms of learning [domains]—cognitive (knowledge), psychomotor (skills), and affective (feelings and attitudes)."[9]

Phillips wrote:

A student who sings learns about life. The transmission of cultural heritages, traditions, and beliefs are all part of the singing experience....To study singing is to study the world. Every student has a right to develop this skill; it is basic for an educated people who desire that each succeeding generation be led to developing a high degree of musical understanding.[10]

---

[9] Ibid., 106.
[10] Ibid.

Phillips describes five broad curriculum goals (listed below), focusing on the basics needed for successful singing. These goals are aligned with the foundations and principles for the mechanics of singing. Each goal is followed by several recommended exercises and activities for students to employ. Together, respiration, phonation, tone production, diction, and expression help students improve.

Respiration
Posture development
- Students require consistent instruction and modeling in correct singing posture, in both a sitting position and standing position.

Breathing motion
- During inhalation, "the diaphragm descends and the lower ribs expand outward, with a corresponding enlargement of the body around the waistline." Likewise, during exhalation, "the diaphragm relaxes and the lower ribs contract inward, with a corresponding contraction of the body around the waistline."[11]

Breath management
- Breath support provides the "power behind the act of singing." Managing air as it supports the sound is a physiological event students should incorporate while singing.

Phonation
Vocal registration (high, middle, low register)
- Phillips adheres to the theory that there are three registrations apparent in the child singing voice. The upper adjustment refers to the head voice. It is normally light and clear in quality, with a ringing quality. The lower adjustment corresponds to the lower, or speaking, voice. The middle voice is a combination of the upper and lower adjustments.

Vocal coordination through registration
- As Phillips stated, "The objective is to smooth over the break between the lower and upper adjustments, creating a smooth passage between."[12]

---

[11] Ibid., 195.
[12] Ibid., 247.

Tone Production

Vocal resonance

- A beautiful voice is one that is "rich in resonance." It is normally characteristic in singers who use their facial muscles to shape the sound forward and bright, and who have a concept of having a round, full tone.

Vowel production

- Phillips reminded readers that vowels "form the basis of resonant tone production." Vowel placement—in the mouth, with the lips and tongue—must be tuned "so as to achieve the most resonant sound and in-tune singing."[13]

---

[13] Ibid., 276.

Diction
Articulation, pronunciation

- While vowels supply the color of the tone, articulating the words with proper diction provides the rhythmic drive and meaning to the text. Beautiful tones mean little if the audience can't understand what the children are conveying textually.

Expression
Phrasing, dynamic and tempo variation, agility

- Good singing is more than clarity of vowels and consonants. It involves bringing musical shape, form, and line to what is sung. Musicianship should be evident in choral singing groups, regardless of their age.

The Mission: Beautiful Singing, Informed Musicianship

McRae wrote:

Singing is an action of the whole body as well as the mind.... The perception of the voice as an instrument is more than a physical image. It is a useful way of depersonalizing singing, which is subject to inhibitions and defensiveness. Treating the voice as an instrument is objective and less threatening.[14]

The vocal instrument, with young and old, requires certain functions working together to yield positive results. These functions must be taught and reinforced within each and every singing activity. Indeed, the goal is for each of the fundamentals mentioned above to become habits employed when students sing.

Dr. Tim Lautzenheiser wrote, "We know that bad habits are easy to form but hard to live with, while good habits are hard to form but easy to live with."[15] This is certainly true when establishing habits related to singing. Developing the students' inclination to immediately implement appropriate posture, supported tone, facial expression, and mouth formation as a matter of habit takes practice, reinforcement, more

---

[14] McRae, 133.
[15] Tim Lautzenheiser, *Everyday Wisdom for Inspired Teaching* (Chicago: GIA Publications, Inc., 2006) 74.

practice, and personal recognition of how improved the sound is as a result of basics.

When a public school children's chorus incorporates foundations for a best sound, there is a distinctive musical quality heard that is unique from miscellaneous voices brought together without instruction in vocal fundamentals. Habits of good singing practices kick in and result in excellent choral tone.

Swears described that a fine children's chorus has the following vocal characteristics and tendencies:

- Use of head voice (a light, forward tone)
- Diction is clear
- Individual voices are blended
- Singing is expressive and conveys the mood and meaning of the words
- Phrasing and vocal line are smooth
- Intonation is accurate[16]

These characteristics are possible to achieve within the general music classroom if deemed a priority by the teacher. It does require consistency and a belief that vocal instruction is worth the time. It also requires that the music educator speak frankly and informatively on what is heard and how the singing can be improved.

---

[16] Swears, 52.

In my research of outstanding children's choir directors, individuals spoke of the need for an education in vocal technique. One director noted:

> I totally believe you can't expect to have a fine children's choir if you're not working on vocal technique in the group. My methodology is that first they have to work on some relaxation, making them understand the importance of posture, then moving to learning about controlled breathing for singing. There's simply no way you work with a group without intense concentration on the shaping of the vowel; that work in itself creates a blend that otherwise would not be there. Children need to know these things in order to sing well. It should be clear that children are work-horses, if they know what they're doing is leading toward excellence.[17]

Students appreciate truth. When listening to a classroom or choir of voices, it is vital for the music educator to avoid meaningless accolades when all informed listeners hear out of tune singing. Bartle indicated the only reason a children's choir might sing out of tune is because someone allows them to.[18] Results come when comments reflect what is heard and are followed by what can be done to improve the sound. Language that describes what is heard and seen can be enhanced and expanded to relate what *could* be heard and what *should* be seen.

When a class or the chorus sounds particularly great, I ask individual students to serve as "witnesses," listening rather than singing, taking note of what they see and hear, applauding afterwards. Listening to students describe what is heard and seen brings assessment and feedback to a whole new level.

For intermediate students, peer approval and bravos are incredibly powerful. Student witnesses who tend to be strong singers recognize the level of achievement, while those witnesses whose singing voices are "in progress" can gaze directly at students singing well and summarize what they see employed for success.

In most general music classrooms and elementary school-based children's choirs, students need reminders of how to stand, where to put their hands, and how to use their faces and eyes to articulate and express the words. They need to be

---

[17] Patricia A. Bourne, "Instructional Techniques for Children's Choirs" (Ed.D. diss., Arizona State University, 1990) 58.

[18] Bartle, *Sound Advice.*

reminded, through physical gesture, modeling, and verbal requests, to support the tone with air and strength in the core of their diaphragmatic muscles. Inside my classroom, this occurs just about every time students open their mouths to sing. My assumption and goal is that these reminders will become routine for most and exceptionally clear with the chorus students.

My intent is to develop habits with students that lead to beautiful singing. I want them to remember to take in air appropriately, to shape the tone, to support the sound, to keep their hands away from their faces, to think and listen. Over time, students will hear me say:

> At Canyon Creek, we sing with our feet slightly apart. Our knee and thigh muscles are relaxed but appear supportive, our hands are relaxed and at our sides, we are standing proud, our shoulders are tall but relaxed, our faces have a "good morning!" alertness. When we sing, we support the sound with a purposeful breath, with intent to pronounce words clearly and shape the vowels with our mouth. We attempt to sing with a musical tone, conveying the song's meaning with our facial expression.

The "good morning!" alertness is particularly fun to work on: I ask students to slump and say, "I'm tired," followed immediately by a perky "Good morning!" That's the look I want in their eyes; that's the energy I want them to feel with their body.

I believe in developing a culture and community of singers at my school. If the community approaches singing with basics in place, beautiful singing will ensue. In the public school music room, teachers will hear a variety of voices; to help those individual voices combine with a common goal—to sing well and sing beautifully—is quite an achievement and one that builds momentum and confidence. It is also habit forming!

Students rise to a level of musicianship when their voices work to perform repertoire written with their (trained) voices in mind. When they hear the results of their efforts, and recognize their vocal achievement, the cycle of singing well becomes the goal and expectation.

Simple Strategies for Evaluating Singing Voices in the Classroom

Developing a group sound is important, but of equal importance are the individual vocal skills and abilities of students. It can take a great deal of time to hear each student sing independently. (One of the many reason most general music

teachers wish for more time with their students, no doubt.) But individual assessment can occur with greater consistency, particularly when you realize that hearing each student does not need to be a grandiose affair. Inside my general music classroom, multiple strategies exist for listening to one voice at a time.

Below is a typical sequence that might last 10 to 15 minutes with a typical class of 26–30 intermediate students. The strategies begin with exploratory sounds within the speaking voice range and end with the singing of a song (i.e. with musical results). (These phases are shown in sample clips in the first part of the DVD.)

Phase One

- Students stand in a circle, all echoing the teacher in vocal inflection and gesture.
- The teacher uses a variety of voices and phrases ("Do your homework!"; "ah...isn't that nice?"; "where are you going?"; "Taxi!"; "Do you like my outfit?") exaggerating gesture as well as volume and vocal directness used.
- After sufficient full-group echoing, the teacher circulates, very quickly, one student to the next, using similar antics. The teacher varies what is used, per student, based on the confidence level and personality of the student she faces.
- Students are encouraged to echo, using the same type of vocal tone/timbre and gesture. It becomes pretty funny at times! In fact, most of my students will say, "Again! Again!" when we do that in a warm-up. If time allows, I will ask a student to be the "teacher," selecting four different phrases to use with four different students.

When I do this activity in my classroom, I will alter the voice that's used according to the perceived abilities of a student. (For instance, if I have a student who tends to sing in a low speaking voice, my spoken phrase to him will actually be placed in a head-tone type sound. I want to know whether he can use that part of his voice.) The teacher is also able to quickly pay attention to each and every child.

Phase Two
- In a circle, students (together) echo teacher, who uses an "oo" vowel with various expressive gestures (e.g, making the "oo" sound like a surprise, a mystery, a disappointment, a secret, etc.).
- As above, each student echoes the teacher as she moves student to student around the circle—quickly! The voice can use *glissando* or definite pitches; it can be short in duration or long and drawn out.
- Once again, gestures accompany the type of "oo" modeled.
- Perceptions and feedback are offered by the teacher as she moves from student to student.

Phase Three
- Back to the whole group—in a circle—students echo more defining pitches, using the "oo" vowel (two-, three-, or four-note short, melodic, legato phrases) with emphasis on gesture. This time the teacher's gesture is either conductor-like or with arms at the side, the face very expressive, the body tall, the shoulders relaxed in a singing position.
- Once again, the teacher goes student to student with the more definitive "oo," listening to and watching how the student sounds and what he does.

If a student does not mimic the singing posture, I'll quickly remind him to use that next time and move on. Drawing attention to someone who's not too secure as a singer is not what this exercise is about: It's to provide me with information. On a second time around, I'll note how the student has incorporated what I suggested, and if the pitch is still off, I will give him another thing to change (there are multiple variables as to what might cause the out-of-tune singing). I will also alter my pitch to be closer to the student's, so that he can hear when it matches. It's crucial to pay attention to body language and move on before any hint of discomfort sets in. These assessment activities work if the teacher adjusts her interactions with each student, according to comfort levels.

When a student matches the pitch with proper singing posture and exquisite tone, I will evaluate how confident he feels showing the class. Student models are my number-one source for helping other students sing in tune. I'll ask students to take over my role, something the advanced, secure singers welcome.

Phase Four

- Introduce or review a short, melodic song with the students while they stand in a circle.
- If teaching this song for the first time, sing the whole song and ask specific questions about what students heard. (E.g. Is it in a foreign language? What is the range of pitches? Are any sections repeated?)
- Teach the song, if through aural tradition, phrase by phrase—teacher sings phrase, students echo. (Teacher does not sing echo with students.)
- Once the song is learned, sing the whole song with students, then ask students to sing independent of teacher. As the song becomes more familiar (over a few lessons), the teacher can begin to enhance the music through instrumental accompaniment, adding harmony, etc.
- Attention is given to appropriate singing gesture—expressive face, support in body and breath, shaping of the vowels and articulation of consonants, etc. As needed, the teacher interjects instructional comments, reminding students of basic principles to be applied.

As the song becomes more secure, it will also be sung with greater proficiency. That's when I invite one or two students to the center of the circle to hear the musical sounds coming from their classmates. That kind of connection between students is extremely powerful, if phased in appropriately and deliberately.

When the class sings a song all know, I will often ask the students to pretend they are being evaluated merely on how they utilize posture, air, formation of the mouth for vowels, and expression in the face and eyes. I'll ask that they pretend they are striving for an A (or above and beyond "standard"). Based on what is seen, comments are offered that reflect what they are doing that would surely earn a high grade. Singing will follow, with posture, breath support, and expressiveness employed, followed by comments of what is heard. It is most powerful to involve students in evaluating the difference supported singing makes.

Emphasis placed on what is seen and heard ignites the ears and eyes of students. Responding to questions like, "How can we improve that phrase?" "What would make the sound brighter?" "Did you remember to take in positive air?" "Are you placing your voice in and out of your forehead?" "Did you use your 'good morning!' eyes?" is all part of the assessment process.

Questioning, reminding, modeling, providing sequential approaches to in-tune singing leads to music-making. I want the students to process what they are doing that either makes it "sound" or makes it musical. They do recognize the difference, given the chance to explain it.

The sound of a well-prepared, secure, confident, and musically sensitive child singer is unlike any other sound source. Children should not sound like adults. They have their own timbre based on multiple factors and variables. Among the most important of variables is the heart and soul of the student: Attention must be given to the spirit of the individual child when directing instructional advice.

General music teachers have the responsibility, and the opportunity, to guide all of their students toward profound singing experiences. This occurs through a variety of reinforcement statements and habit-forming routines. It is possible to move all students forward. For some, this occurs quickly, seamlessly, and with wonderful overt changes in the student's attitude and level of participation. For others, patience must be employed.

Herrington encourages teachers to "go the extra mile" in developing the "artistic hearts of singers."[19] Bartle added, "Despite the conditions in which we may find ourselves, music

---

[19] Judith Herrington, "Mission Possible – Children Can Sing Beautifully" (paper presented at the ArtsTime Conference, Tukwila, Washington, March 2003).

will continue to be one of the greatest gifts to humanity, perhaps *the* greatest. We must never sell it short."[20]

Listen to and watch your students. <u>Once a song is learned, stop singing</u> with the students. You can hear how they really sound. Build their confidence and independence. Develop a singing culture within your classrooms. Describe what you want to see and hear; be ready to repeat that message as many times as it takes to become habit. Look for student leaders and student models.

The rewards of listening to children sing well overwhelm the day-after-day, week-after-week reminders you employ. Don't give up!

[20] Bartle, *Sound Advice*, 90.

Membership in the Non-Select Chorus

Folk singer and songwriter Bill Staines wrote a song titled "A Place in the Choir" indicating all the "critters" are welcome to join and have a purpose for participating. To a certain degree, that's the attitude to consider when making decisions on who will or won't be accepted or invited into the elementary children's choir. Phillips cautioned:

> One of the dangers of the elementary school choral program, if not handled correctly, is it may tend to foster the idea of musical 'elitism' at an age when just the opposite should be occurring. In their desire to produce superior musical results, music teachers leave children out of choral organizations [because of] audition expectations....Being chosen or not chosen for the elementary chorus may very well carry with the label of singer or non-singer. All children should have equal opportunities to grow musically.[1]

While I agree students should have equal *access* to the public school chorus, I most heartily recommend that the general music teacher/chorus director establish specific criteria for membership. Otherwise, the group can easily become one that is a "come when it's convenient" ensemble rather than one with student, parent, and classroom teacher investment and commitment.

At Canyon Creek, 5th- and 6th-grade students are *invited* to membership based on four criteria:

---

[1] Phillips, 17.

1. While singing, obvious attempts are made to improve. The student accepts and applies advice for improved vocal tone.
2. The student is able to manage his or her own behavior, allowing me to teach without disruption. (Since the Canyon Creek Chorus tends to be large, this ability is crucial.)
3. The student completes the signatures necessary for full membership—his or her own, parents', and classroom teacher's.
4. The student is able to attend rehearsals (at least a majority of them) and does not foresee any conflicts with performance dates.

I did not use a contract during my first years as a public school general music teacher/children's choir director. I assumed a volunteer chorus would be something the students would commit to and attend on a regular basis, arriving on time and ready to rehearse, ready to participate completely, ready to give up their recess time to practice. That worked for about 65% of the kids; the others figured it might be okay to go outside to play, or it might be okay to skip chorus since the purpose of rehearsal was not made evident to them. The "ya'll come" chorus did not work for me! I needed something to inspire buy-in, commitment, and evidence that students understood what they were choosing to be a part of. And because contracts are distributed and returned two weeks before rehearsals commence, students have plenty of time to consider membership. (See pages 64–65 for a sample letter of invitation and contract. Samples of chorus newsletters and other communiqués also follow at the end of this chapter.)

Once the contract was employed, attendance was vastly better. In addition, student behavior during rehearsals improved. I was not waiting for a parent to pick up his or her child long after dismissal. Classroom teachers became cheerleaders for those choosing to be in the group. Everyone seemed to understand and accept the necessity for rehearsal attendance. There was an immediate and positive improvement to the overall membership and feeling tone of the group. Best of all, I enjoyed the benefits of commitment.

One of the immediate benefits of the contract was the evidence I had in my possession of the students' promise to participate to the best of their ability. As the contract indicates, students understand that they are responsible for their actions and will give careful attention to their learning and the learning of others. When chorus members "forget" that part of the deal, I reach for their contract and show what they promised to do, with their signature as proof. That simple action takes care of most behavioral issues, quickly and succinctly.

I made the decision to not include a vocal audition for chorus membership, knowing full well the drawbacks to using non-musical criteria only. When people listen to the Canyon Creek Chorus, they do not hear perfect intonation from all members 100% of the time. They *do*, however, hear children who've learned positive techniques of choral singing and are applying them in rehearsal and performance. They hear children who have elected to invest their free time in improved musicianship. Finally, audiences recognize and appreciate the code of conduct displayed before, during, and after performances.

Since singing in tune is not a prerequisite for membership, the chorus has children who are in a "progressing toward singing in tune" mode of operation. With consistent exercises and warm-ups specifically designed for those children, plus placement around others who do sing well, they improve. These students were invited to membership due to their attitude toward singing and consistent attempts to improve; in my opinion, their membership should be prized and appreciated as much as those with stunning voices.

Each children's choir director has the right to establish criteria that best suit her goals for the ensemble. For example, interviews with numerous directors granted preferred selection of choristers through a vocal audition coupled with non-musical criterion. Specifically, potential members had to demonstrate competency in:

1. Singing in tune
2. Demonstrating rhythmic discrimination and ability to maintain beat
3. Singing back patterns (i.e., tonal memory)
4. Singing with a healthy tone (no physiological impairments)

Non-musical criteria included:

1. Demonstrating an effort and willingness to try
2. Receiving and acting on instructions
3. Displaying a positive attitude, especially toward learning
4. Staying on task
5. Displaying social readiness and developmental maturity

In a public school, the music teacher usually makes decisions affecting the school climate with input from other key personnel. If the chorus is to become part of a school's identity, those welcomed or unwelcomed into membership have direct implications and consequences on the rest of the school. I believe teachers elicit stronger support for a choral program when input is invited, particularly from those who affect the student's life (parents, classroom teachers, building administrator, etc.). Involving others in decisions will have a direct effect on the reception and acceptance of chorus as a performing entity.

Although I personally made the decision to control membership through non-musical criteria only, knowing that my colleagues and administrator supported that decision made it seem right for all of us. I strongly agree with a statement by Swears regarding membership in the public school elementary chorus:

The elementary chorus should be as inclusive as possible, never excluding a child because he or she doesn't sing well. All children need as much singing experience as possible and can benefit greatly from the attention placed on vocal skills in the school chorus. Telling a child he or she may not participate in chorus because he or she does not sing well is a sure way to stifle further vocal development....The overall attitude in chorus should be one that encourages all children to do their best while accepting and helping one another.[2]

When asked whether a vocal audition is required for membership in the Canyon Creek 5th/6th-Grade Chorus, I direct potential new members (and their parents) to the chorus link on my school's Web site (ccweb.nsd.org). The primary question regarding membership and its answer are as follows:

Does a student need to audition or sing, by themselves, in front of the teacher and/or class?

As a part of the general music class, students sing: They sing together, they sing in small groups, they echo simple tunes from the teacher. Mrs. Bourne will not make a reluctant singer sing; however, the fact that someone will not willingly allow themselves to improve as a singer indicates a lack of desire to be invited to join the chorus. Out-of-tune voices are not a problem! Less than 1% of the population is truly tone deaf. More often, individuals have not been taught to use their singing voice correctly. Singing is most definitely a learned behavior! Students are asked to give it their best shot. A voice that is currently "out of tune" is not a major issue—an unwillingness to try or attitude to not learn is.

Membership Realities: From the Students

Recently, I asked several veteran members of the Canyon Creek Chorus to explain why they elected to join another year. Answers ranged from "It's fun; you get to have a great time" to "A bunch of my friends joined again" to "I really like those field trips we take" to "I'd rather be with my friends than at home watching TV." One student said, "Well, if you like music the way I do, this is just a natural thing to do." A few indicated their enjoyment of singing was the impetus for joining, but most answers were friendship-oriented.

Does that create a problem? The truth is, kids normally enjoy each other's company. They also enjoy a good time, even when focus and effort is expected. I most sincerely believe students who join primarily for social reasons have not nega-

---

[2] Swears, 17.

tively affected membership in the Canyon Creek Chorus. On
the contrary, the friendship factor is a powerful ally, as long as
everyone understands the intent, purpose, and code of conduct within the group. I'm fairly certain that several students
would've thought twice about membership in the group had
they not seen friends taking part.

Sullo noted that pre-adolescent children have a desire to
please, but "the reference point becomes the peer group, not
parents and teachers. They are concerned about how others
see them and work diligently to gain approval."[3] Boys, in particular, want to be "100 percent convinced that they will be
successful within the group before trying it."[4]

At my school, students invited to chorus have proven their
ability to be with friends and maintain self-discipline. They
show, through their commitment to the group (as witnessed
by their signature on the contract), that they understand this
ensemble exists with a clearly defined mission. If a student
accepts the invitation to join primarily due to whom else is
joining, I do not have a problem with that! The long-term

[3] Robert A. Sullo, *The Inspiring Teacher: New Beginnings for the 21st
Century* (Washington D.C.: National Education Association, 1999) 80.
[4] Peter A. Eklund, "25 Tips for Engaging Male Singers," *Choral
Director* 1, no. 2 (winter 2004): 10.

benefits of participation are evident in the number of students choosing to continue performance options after they leave the elementary setting. My goal is that they grow to enjoy participation in choir for musical reasons and seek future opportunities to be involved.

Boys! Getting Them, Keeping Them

Several years ago, I was invited to apply for artistic director of a professional girls' choir existing in our area. While flattered by this invitation, I couldn't imagine directing an ensemble without boys; their membership contributes a kind of energy, humor, bravado, and even edginess I would miss in an all-girls group. It's the combination of boy and girl learners/musicians that is appealing to me. The mixture of chemistry is instructionally fascinating!

In his article "25 Tips for Engaging Male Singers," Eklund wrote that girls are "smart enough to sign up [for organizations] on their own; girls will often experiment and try something if they think they might enjoy it."[5] Boys are another matter. They operate under a code that distinguishes what is manly and what might be interpreted as girlish and will err on the side of doubt.[6]

It's the director's job to showcase the choral ensemble as a group for girls *and* boys. If the director is also the general music teacher, she has multiple opportunities to teach in ways that are motivating and appropriate for boys, thus planting the seed that the chorus will not be a "sissy" undertaking. From activities within the general music curricula to choices in song material, the teacher can provide instruction that is "boy friendly."

Boys need movement. They need hands-on projects. They have a biological need for motion and learn best when given opportunities for movement during the school day. They invest in learning when the topic is of interest to them and calls for active involvement. Normally, general music classes fulfill these learning requirements.

---

[5] Ibid.
[6] Terry W. Neu and Rich Weinfeld, *Helping Boys Succeed in School* (Waco, TX: Prufrock Press, Inc., 2007).

Inside most general music classrooms, students are active participants in moving, playing, listening, writing, improvising, working with others on group compositions, and are engaged kinesthetically. It's an optimal place to teach to the boy brain. Girls like the motion as well, but don't seem to *need* it quite as desperately as the fellows.

When boys experience success in the general music classroom, they develop fewer inhibitions to be involved in music elsewhere. They tend to believe the teacher traits shown in one environment will be used in another; that is, if they are engaged and interested and motivated and involved in general music, why would chorus be any different if led by the same educator?

In my effort to establish a singing culture with the classes I teach, every effort is made to celebrate the sounds heard from all singers; however, if I'm trying to build the confidence and participation level of the boys in the room, I will involve them more directly through active participation. We step the beat while singing, we conduct, we alter expressive components of a song we're singing to stimulate the brain. We add instrumental accompaniment to enhance the sound, when appropriate repertoire-wise. Students are reminded to use their muscles as well as their minds. Physical gestures will be used to remind students that singing is a physical activity. In my classroom, singing is doing, and all doers sing!

Eklund wrote teachers and directors should consider what's going on inside the mind of a potential male singer. The typical ten- to twenty-year-old male who's considering chorus as a possible activity will think:

> Do not make me feel uncomfortable or I'll find somewhere else to be.

> Do not stick to one kind of music and don't program easy "fluff" music. Do not give all of your attention to the good singers.[7]

The author recommended that teachers/directors consider using non-musical incentives for joining a choral ensemble, like pizza or prizes. It doesn't have to be big, but boys do seem to operate differently when they believe they'll be fed! He stated:

---

[7] Eklund, 12.

- Arrange for tours and field trips; opportunities to go off campus
- Select attire that is becoming of young men
- Feature boys in concerts (this can include musical as well as non-musical features. I am always amazed how thrilled my older boys are to set up the risers for performances.)
- Make chorus the thing to do at your school by having returning boy members recruit new boy members (Boys tend to be drawn to those activities that have strong "boy presence." If a director wants to recruit new boys to the choral ensemble, utilizing returning boys is far more powerful than a flyer or poster. Boys will go with a sure bet, and if their buddies are involved, that inspires them to join.)
- Attend events that your boys are involved with: track meets, soccer games, football games, etc. (At our school, the head custodian teaches table tennis during an afterschool activity time. At the conclusion of the six-week class, staff members are invited to take on the 5th- and 6th-grade players. That level of involvement is an opportune time to engage the mostly boy group in a friendly sporting adventure).
- Look for something new and unique to keep the kids talking about choir in a positive way.[8]

---

[8] Ibid., 11.

I once met a first-year teacher who was hired to direct both the band and chorus at a middle school. The initial enrollment in the 8th-grade chorus was 15 girls, no boys. As a nationally ranked wrestler and college football player, this teacher was also hired as assistant football coach, spending a week prior to the school year working with the team. During football camp, he listened to the boys during lunch and during free time, identifying the various ranges of voices heard. He challenged several to sign up for chorus, mentioning how "real singers" have amazing abdominal muscles. Due to his stature and relationship with the boys, he was able to say, "Fellows, real men sing." By October, membership in the 8th-grade chorus included the original 15 girls along with nine boys. By the following year, numbers had doubled. This gentleman knew how to use his resources!

Last year, I asked quite a few of my boy chorus members what inspired them to join. Answers varied from those given above, but only slightly. It usually came back to "my friends were in it." One boy said, "When I was little, I knew a 6th-grade guy I thought was pretty cool. So, when I saw him singing in chorus, I immediately saw it as something cool guys do." One fast-growing boy admitted, in jest, "I knew we'd get snacks now and then and eating is something I love to do, regardless of where I am or what I'm doing!"

Boys must see chorus as an active and positive organization to be a part of, not just in elementary school, but also beyond. Each November, I ask members of the high school jazz choir to come to one of our rehearsals to watch, listen, and perform for us. With eight young men and women standing before the 5th and 6th graders, I watch my boys connect with the bearded, deep-voiced 17 and 18 year olds singing for them. They understand that, in a short while, they will be that size. More importantly, they begin to grasp the idea that singing continues throughout their schooling. (I'm exceptionally indebted to our high school choral director and her students—they have made an enormous impact on my young singers. I must admit, it's especially fulfilling to see Canyon Creek alumni performing with this superb vocal ensemble).

Questions to Consider Regarding Membership

Starting a children's chorus within a public school requires some advance planning, particularly if the general music teacher intends to *enjoy* the experience with those members who elect to participate. Recently, I talked with a group of young teachers who were getting ready to begin choruses at their respective public schools. Several questions emerged during our conversation that are worth sharing:

How do I decide what grade level(s) to include?

The typical elementary school encompasses grades K–5 or K–6. Obviously the population within those grades can fluctuate school to school, affecting the available personnel for choir members. In my elementary choirs, upper grades were involved due to their sheer numbers (anywhere from 80 to 175 students). While a smaller school might yield fewer students from which to draw, I strongly urge teachers to consider offering chorus to grade levels that are somewhat similar developmentally and vocally.

For the most part, I want my chorus members to be:

- Physically capable of singing more comfortably with a wide range of pitches
- Able to exercise personal accountability normally anticipated and expected of older elementary students

- Similar in reading and reasoning skills so that the questions I ask and the instructional pacing of our one hour together can be streamlined
- Able to sing standard choral repertoire normally written for students with more maturing voices (pre-adolescent treble)

According to Swears, the vocal range of older elementary children expands with more clarity throughout the voice and purity in the upper register. "By 5th and 6th grade, students reach the peak of vocal development: A child's physical, intellectual, and emotional maturation work together to foster expressive singing."[9] As a result of their physical maturation, the respiratory systems of children become more adult-like around age 11, "so at that time more dynamic as well as phrasing possibilities can be considered."[10] Students in and around the age of 10 to 12 have the stamina and sustaining power to sing a broad range of repertoire more expressively than young children.

In short, the general music teacher should decide what the overall objectives and goals are for the school's children's chorus and narrow the grades to fit those objectives. All veteran teachers understand the trials of multi-age instruction when

---

[9] Swears, 25.
[10] Trollinger, 22.

students span more than three or four years in age, particularly at the elementary level. If a good-size school population exists, I would suggest restricting membership to your oldest two grade levels: The sound will be less diverse and the instructional strategies will be developmentally specific. It will also provide the younger children with something to look forward to.

A few teachers I know offer a primary or training chorus that is more like a music club than a performing ensemble. The grade levels are closely linked (2nd and 3rd graders, for instance) and provide a place for children of similar age and developmental levels to explore singing together beyond the general music classroom.

How many student members make an ideal-sized public school group?

I once met a general music teacher who maintained a fifty-voice choir at her school. Regardless of eligible numbers, fifty students was the membership level she was comfortable with. When asked why, she indicated that her effectiveness as teacher, director, and organizer of the group was strained with more than 50 chorus members. This teacher made decisions that helped her maintain a manageable ensemble, size wise. Years of experience and enjoyment as children's choir director helped define her ideal size.

Since the criteria for membership in my public school chorus is based on non-musical criteria, roughly 98% of the population receives an invitation to join. A typical year will yield 50% to 60% of the school's population of 5th and 6th graders choosing to accept the invitation to participate. The number has varied over the past fourteen years, but is usually around 80 students.

The number of student singers does affect the organization, communication, and logistics of the ensemble. In the end, the director, along with other potential decision makers (administrator, etc.), establishes membership with consideration of the director's time, inclination for working with large (or small) groups, and the overall goals of the organization.

How do I accommodate our special education population and design an inclusive elementary chorus?

With the onset of legislation mandating the accessibility of a public school education for all students, the inclusion of special education students became an ever-expanding reality. The addition of diverse learners within general music classes continues to grow, as do the resources available for teachers to implement curricula that best serves cognitively, developmentally, and physically challenged children.

The Americans with Disabilities Act (ADA) provides broad civil rights protection for individuals with disabilities. "All students must have access to classes and ensembles that are available to the general school population."[11] According to the law, if students aren't allowed to participate in ensembles or general music classes that are generally open to other students then the school is likely violating the intent of ADA.

Most general music teachers have multiple strategies that help guide instruction in diversely populated classrooms. Those with choral ensembles must do the same without compromising the success of the larger population of students. In conjunction with our special education staff, each student is considered individually with chorus membership in mind. Can they self-manage? Do their parents support membership in the group? Have they displayed an interest in singing and participated as appropriately as their disability allows within the general music class? If I answer yes to any of those questions, an invitation is extended and adaptations are made so that they may be successful.

Once a special education child commits to membership in the chorus, accommodations for his or her full participation are put in place. Will an aide need to be present during rehearsals, performances, and field trips? Where should the student(s) be positioned to draw strength, support, and a degree of empathy from other chorus members? What expectations should I, as director, extend to the children with particular challenges?

One of my routines each year is to create recordings of our music that the students can use when practicing at home. Our accompanist receives the selections and, when ready, comes to

---

[11] Kimberly McCord and Emily H. Watts, "Collaboration and Access for our Children: Music Education and Special Educators Together," *Music Educators Journal* 92, no. 4 (2006): 26.

the music room where I record the piano part into a simple program (I use GarageBand). Later, I add the vocal tracks, export the recording to iTunes, and burn CDs.[12] Now standard, this practice began as an aid for special-needs children who were unable to read the words and needed more repetition than our once-a-week rehearsal times afforded.

Our chorus has been enriched by its members—*all* of its members. Not once have I regretted extending an invitation to children with challenges. A few have stood with the group, smiling broadly not singing a note due to the visual stimulation of audience and light and sound, yet their commitment to the ensemble was easily felt and appreciated.

What are simple strategies for advertising membership in the chorus?

Once hired to a general music position, a teacher becomes familiar with the ebb and flow of the school very quickly. She will have a good sense of how, when, and with whom to talk regarding the establishment of a school chorus. Once the decision is made to move forward with a choral ensemble, it's time to devise recruitment and advertising strategies.

Obviously, sharing information during general music classes is an ideal way to start. Students will want to know what the chorus will do and why it's worth their time to join. Students tend to avoid that which appears boring; therefore, before advertising the chorus, have something in place that is new, exciting, enticing, and motivating. Field trips are wonderful motivators (especially those that occur during the school day).

Since chorus is a continuing afterschool activity in our school, I usually prepare an updated PowerPoint presentation with pictures of members enjoying their time together—in rehearsal, in performance, eating food at concert receptions. I also ask second-year students to "talk up chorus" with other 5th and 6th graders. I particularly rely on my second-year boys to recruit other boys. Finally, I mention chorus in newsletters sent to 5th- and 6th-grade parents.

I've learned simple flyers and one-time announcements usually yield a limited number of respondents. I approach students individually and collectively, letting them know of the benefits of membership, socially and musically. Once, I told two boys (who sang beautifully in class) that I'd be tempted to buy them

---

[12] Pre-recorded practice tracks may also be available, but if you elect to make your own be sure to get permission from the publisher.

each an ice cream sundae in return for membership. Membership of boys was a tad low that year and these guys were "alphas"—other boys looked up to them. By golly, it worked! The number of boys joining increased dramatically after these two boys did. Well worth the price of a Dairy Queen sundae token!

Public school children's chorus members commit to the group based on their relationship with the teacher/director and other students in the group. As students hand in their chorus contracts, I post names on the bulletin board outside the music room. Students will glance at the names and see folks they recognize and are friends with. Peer involvement is a powerful motivator—announce it!

Finally, constructing and contributing to the school's Web site is helpful. More and more of our 5th- and 6th-grade teachers utilize their classroom sites to communicate directly with parents and students. Asking the teachers to place a link to the music Web site can be very effective.

Should I investigate a preferred rehearsal time with potential members before I post when the chorus will meet?

Depending on the size of your group, you will want to find a time that is best available for those involved. However, it's *impossible* to find a time that works for all. Finding a time that does not conflict with existing clubs/organizations within the school is important. Obviously, scheduling a time that works consistently for the director and other personnel (particularly your accompanist) is imperative.

From my experience, I know that recesses are really tough on attendance—avoid them if you can. Besides that, children need to play. They need to run. This is particularly important with older elementary students, who tend to not play the games or climb the play toys of younger children. Giving up a full lunch period is also tough, as preadolescent children need opportunities to practice the social interactions usually allowed during lunch. Pull-out programs (those where specific members of a classroom leave while other remain) for elementary chorus are a true rarity. While supportive classroom teachers surround me, their days are packed and time with students is crucial for curricular necessities, making a pull-out system an unreasonable request at my school.

I would not expect them to give up essential instructional time for chorus rehearsal, regardless of their level of support.

Before- and afterschool groups encounter transportation issues. While a vast majority of our students ride school buses, we do have parents willing to collect their children (and other neighborhood children) when chorus dismisses a full hour and 20 minutes after the school day ends. Carpools are organized and some students sit and finish homework while waiting for a working parent to arrive. Parents are key to successful before- or after-school programs; without them, our group could not exist!

I recommend talking with the building administrator and classroom teachers before selecting rehearsal times. Once the time is selected, be consistent—try to keep that time frame as sacred and protected as possible.

I'm considering establishing an auditioned group. What, if any, unique challenges will I face?

General music teachers who elect to proceed with an auditioned chorus must establish clear lines of communication with all parties involved. It is critical to establish a trusting rapport with all constituents—students, parents, the building administrator, and classroom teachers—so that the selectivity exercised is supported and understood.

The choice to hold vocal auditions and to select elementary students based on their vocal abilities alone is not something I would encourage. Intermediate-level elementary students need a variety of experiences to find their "place" and strengths. The thought of a child having the courage to audition for a public school ensemble and then being told he or she does not sing well enough to join is philosophically opposed to my belief of the purpose for a public school children's chorus.

I believe feelings will be hurt, personal perceptions of singing ability will be altered, and students will avoid trying again. There are a number of community-based professional choruses that have stringent vocal auditions, but the children not accepted are not placed in a classroom twice a week with the adult who figuratively indicated, "You're just not good enough." For those public school music educators who choose to pursue an auditioned group, I strongly encourage the exercising of great care in audition and invitation procedures.

Should I offer some kind of incentive for signing up for chorus?

Initially, some kind of "carrot" could be a good idea, particularly if the ensemble is a new addition to the school's culture. As you've read, food is a tremendous motivator. Students tell their friends about the surprise treat given at the first rehearsal. (I usually distribute lollipops after the first or second rehearsal together, showing them how they can practice their vowels with the variety of ways one can enjoy a big, round sucker. The kids love it and tell their friends about it.) They look forward to traditional activities included from time-to-time within the rehearsal structure.

When chorus becomes something 5th and 6th graders "do" at the school, the ensemble has entered the realm of reflecting the culture and heart of the school itself. Being a member of chorus is often incentive enough, especially when it provides an identity, purpose, and service to the school.

Establishing a Choral Identity

Members of the elementary public school chorus tend to reflect the diversity of the school itself. If the chorus is part of the identity and culture of the community, it will embrace children with various learning styles and motives for belonging to the group. Regardless of vocal acuity or maturity of physique, students involved in the choral ensemble should share a common purpose: they want to be there and they want to help the group succeed.

Although the sound of a non-auditioned public school choir may not reach the musical artistry of a highly select professional group, the attitude and commitment level of the individuals involved should not be compromised. The director has the right to establish criteria for membership, thus shaping the identity of her group.

Our identity at Canyon Creek is simple and linked to our motto: "Stand proud, sing proud, look proud, be proud." I want the kids to leave rehearsals telling their parents details of what they helped accomplish. I want them walking into rehearsal with an anticipation that they are a part of something terrific and important. I want the chorus to become part of their identity while members of the ensemble and school community.

Likewise, the group becomes an identity unto itself. We have a sound that we're working toward. We work toward a sense of professionalism that guides behavior. We have faith in each other's commitment and sense of responsibility to the group. While this optimistic perception varies in degree from student to student, there is a feeling tone generated during our rehearsals and performances that is detectable and obvious to observers.

I am proud to be the director of a choral ensemble that accepts each other and has elected to work toward a common goal. I'll take kids like that any day.

To: **Fifth and Sixth Grade Students and Parents**
From: **Mrs. Bourne, Music Teacher at Canyon Creek**
Re: **Chorus Information and Contract**
Date: **September 10, 2008**

It is my pleasure to invite you to membership in the Canyon Creek 5th/6th-Grade Chorus. This group has been in existence for 12 years, and has performed at state and regional music conferences, appeared on TV while performing at the Four Seasons Hotel, entertained district administrators, sung at Benaroya Hall in Seattle, and participated in Winterfest at the Seattle Center. The goal of the chorus is to sing a wide variety of music and to represent Canyon Creek and Northshore School District through stellar performances, courteous behavior, and thoughtful artistry.

In order to perform as well as possible, rehearsals are necessary! The chorus will rehearse after school, on *Wednesdays, beginning September 19.* Students will be asked to gather in the gym for practice; those who serve as safety patrol or bus monitors will be expected to arrive in the gym as soon as their responsibilities are finished. Dismissal will occur at 4:20 P.M. Since it is after school, students and parents will need to work together to determine how singers will be transported home. *I strongly encourage carpooling!*

Performances will occur in December and March. Our final concert of the year will be during the second week of March. *Chorus will end after that.* Students will perform wearing black on the bottom and white on the top. It's important that our look be as terrific as our sound. (More information on this will arrive in the first chorus newsletter.)

If you decide to join chorus, here's what needs to occur:

1. Complete the contract, found on the back of this page, and turn it in to Mrs. Bourne soon. Contracts must be turned in before the first rehearsal, otherwise the student does not have permission to remain at school.
2. Make plans to remain at school each and every Wednesday until 4:20.
3. Decide how students will get home following rehearsals.
4. Prepare your mind, body, and voice for some great music making!

If you are returning to chorus for a second year, you will be expected to serve as a role model for new members. You will be asked to demonstrate what it looks like to focus, to be responsible for yourselves and each other, and to be tolerant of those around you. The chorus should build friendships and relationships—it is based on mutual trust and high expectations. Besides that, it's fun! (...especially the field trips!).

Questions? Please do not hesitate to contact Mrs. Bourne

Thank you; I look forward to a wonderful choral season together!

CHORUS CONTRACT
To be returned *before* the first rehearsal.

For the chorus member:

I am choosing to become a member of the Canyon Creek 5th/6th-Grade Chorus. By choosing to do this, I will attend all rehearsals, I will participate to the best of my ability, I will be responsible for my actions, I will represent myself, my family, and my school with courteous behavior, a strong and musical voice, and careful attention to my learning and the learning of others.

Student signature: _____

For the chorus member's parent and/or guardian:

I will support my son/daughter's membership in the chorus by allowing him/her to remain after school on Wednesdays for rehearsals and by the reading the monthly chorus newsletters so that I am informed of the chorus activities. I will be sure that my son/daughter knows how to get home following rehearsals and will provide that information to the director (see below).

Parent or Guardian signature: _____

Please print name: _____

For the chorus member's classroom teacher:

I understand that this student has promised to be a member of the chorus and trust that he/she will abide by the expectations stated for chorus members. Students will be excused from my class for scheduled chorus field trips. If I have concerns about a student's membership, I will contact Mrs. Bourne.

Classroom Teacher signature: _____

- -

Parents, please confirm what your son/daughter is to do following dismissal from chorus rehearsal:

_____ I will pick up my chorus member *promptly* following rehearsal, at 4:20 P.M.

_____ My chorus member will ride home with _____

_____ My chorus member will walk home

_____ Other? Please describe. _____

_____

Chorus News

February/March

We're nearing the end of our season!...

Our final rehearsals are approaching (this Wednesday, February 27 and next Wednesday, March 5). As always, attendance is a must.

PERFORMANCE, Tuesday, March 11, Northshore Performing Arts Center on the Bothell High Campus. This concert is with the choirs from Skyview Jr. High and Bothell High School.

GET PERFORMANCE ATTIRE READY! White dress shirts/blouses. Black on the bottom. Slacks okay for girls. Boys, dress pants, black shoes/socks. Boys may bring their own tie or use one of the chorus's.

Plan to arrive at the venue no later than 6:15 P.M. The concert is free and begins at 7:00. ALL CANYON CREEK STUDENTS WILL RE-MAIN TOGETHER AND LISTEN TO THE OTHER CHOIRS. We will sing in the final combined number and it's essential we stay together in the audience. The concert should conclude by 8:30.

FIELD TRIP to Bothell High School, Tuesday, March 11, 9:00 to 10:30 A.M. If there is a permission slip attached, *please* return it as soon as possible.

THANK YOU, students and parents, for a wonderful concert year. On March 12, I hope to have parts of the DVD that will be included in the book I'm writing (released in the winter of '09) to show. It will be fun to relax, eat, and watch parts of that.

Nov/Dec Chorus Newsletter

PARENTS AND CHORUS MEMBERS:

THANKS to the parents who contributed and served snacks at our special Tuesday rehearsal. They provided a welcome break for our students as well as students from the high school who performed for us that day.

TWO rehearsals remain before our concerts (Wednesday, Nov. 29 and Wednesday, Dec. 5.)

SPEAKING of concerts—the Bothell High School choirs will perform with the high school orchestra on Thursday, December 6. This is a ticketed event ($4.00 for adults, $2.00 for students). This will be a wonderful concert, featuring all the choirs during the first half and Handel's *Messiah* the second half. On December 12, the Skyview Music Department will have their concert in the Skyview gym.

OUR concert is Monday, December 10, at the Northshore Performing Arts Center (on the BHS campus, next to the gym). CHORUS members arrive at 5:45 in order to rehearse in the hall. The concert begins at 7:00 with the BHS Men's Chorus and Jazz Choir. A reception will follow, in the choir room. (Thanks to those parents contributing desserts and helping with the set-up/clean-up.)

FIELD TRIP info! Permission slips are attached. Please complete them, and return to Mrs. Bourne with the $5.50 bus fee included. What a fun trip this will be! Concert attire must be worn.

CONCERT ATTIRE! Please be sure to be outfitted in the appropriate concert attire: Black on the bottom (no jeans), dress white on top (no turtlenecks), black on the feet. If your son needs to borrow a tie, please let Mrs. Bourne know as soon as possible. We're trying to outfit our young men in solid ties (black, blue, red, etc.). Decorative ribbons for our girls will be distributed before each concert.

JANUARY chorus rehearsals begin the first Wednesday back to school. New members may join our current chorus members. I look forward to beginning new songs with the group for our March performances.

ON a personal note, I would like to thank the members of this year's chorus for a tremendous fall. They have tackled every challenge and have treated each other (and me) with kindness, respect, and mutual support. They have worked hard at each rehearsal (even on Halloween!). I'm thrilled with their progress, commitment, and responsibility to the group. I encourage friends, family, and neighbors to hear the chorus on December 10, in the NPAC, and/or on December 11, in the Canyon Creek gym (9:00 A.M.). I'm certain you'll be as impressed as I.

THANK YOU!

Chorus News

LAST REHEARSAL(S) ARE HERE

The last Wednesday rehearsal for the chorus will be February 28, at the regular time in the regular place. We'll close that rehearsal with a short celebration to close the season. We will NOT meet the Wednesdays to follow.

The next day, Thursday, March 1, we will travel by bus to Bothell High School and rehearse with their choir(s) on a piece we sing together. The bus will leave school around 9:00 A.M. and return one hour later.

On Tuesday, March 6, we will have a short gathering and warm-up in the music room during lunch recess, and that evening, students are due at BHS by 6:10 P.M. We will have parents/students posted directing people to the right place. The concert begins at 7:00 P.M. in the Performing Arts Center (on the BHS campus). It will last approximately 1 hour 45 minutes. Be sure to wear black on the bottom, dress white on top, all in black shoes/black socks or tights, ties for the guys (we can supply many with one).

THANK YOU, PARENTS

Thank you, parents, for your support. The chorus would be unable to function if it weren't for families that made commitments and altered schedules to allow participation. I appreciate your sense of service to the school, and the efforts you made to be sure your son/daughter attended rehearsals, dressed appropriately for concerts, and remained committed to the original signed contract. Hopefully, I'll see many returning students in next year's chorus. Enjoy the remainder of your spring!

Chorus Parent Volunteers Needed!

Please look over the list and consider how you might best help. THANKS!
(Place a check mark by any that you might assist with).

NOVEMBER 20, special rehearsal (11:45 A.M. – 1:30 P.M.)

Provide water bottles (one dozen): _____
Provide fruit:
Apple slices: _____
Grapes: _____
Orange slices: _____
Provide cookies: _____
Provide other snack (non-peanut-related): _____

Help setup table and snacks in the back of gym (at 12:35): _____
Help distribute snacks (from 12:45–12:50): _____
Clean up and put away table(s) (at 1:00): _____

DECEMBER 10, evening concert at Northshore Performing Arts Center

Help with ties and ribbons, back stage: _____
Help clean up concert hall
(remaining programs, lost and found, etc.): _____
Help setup reception area (BHS Library): _____
Donate a dessert for the reception (after the concert): _____
Help clean up following reception: _____

DECEMBER 11, field trip to Seattle, 9:10 A.M. – 2:30 P.M.):

Chaperone (MUST HAVE volunteer paperwork
completed and returned!): _____

(We will not have drivers, since we are using school busses for transportation this year. We should have room for about 20 additional adults.)

YOUR CHORUS MEMBER'S NAME: _____

PARENT NAME: _____

BEST WAY TO CONTACT YOU: _____

Repertoire, Materials, and Resources

The decision is made to establish a choral ensemble at your elementary school. Rehearsal times have been scheduled; membership recruitment has begun. Hopefully an accompanist is secured. Communication has occurred between the general music teacher/director and other key constituents in the school (administrator, classroom teachers, parents). Performances are scheduled and on the school calendar. The next question: "Now that I've started a choir, what will they sing?"

Selecting repertoire is an extremely critical piece of the chorus equation. Small wrote, "The best choral experience and the best music education always start with the music."[1] Fortunately for those of us directing children's choirs, quality repertoire is readily available.

Indeed, more and more selections voiced in appropriate ranges are accessible to directors of elementary school children's choirs. According to Small, "Twenty five years ago, beginning choral conductors could voice concerns over the lack of materials for children, or lack of knowledge, or lack of models to which they could listen. Those circumstances no longer exist."[2]

As a public school and community children's choral director for 27 years, I concur with that statement. In my beginning years as director, music choices were slim. More often than not, I included pieces drawn from the school's music textbook series or I would write simple arrangements of public domain songs. Sometimes, I'd choose pieces scored for soprano, alto,

---

[1] Ann Small, "Beginning a Children's Choir: No Dinosaurs Here," *Choral Journal* 47, no. 2 (August 2006) 63.
[2] Ibid., 64.

tenor, and bass and teach my students only the soprano line. However, within the past 15–20 years, children's choir literature has dramatically expanded. Notable composers and arrangers are actively writing for children's voices and extending the genre/stylistic options for their directors.

Planning repertoire is based on clientele and membership in the chorus as well as a host of other variables. General music teachers who recruit and select children for their public school choirs have an advantage: They often know the kinds of voices they will have in the group and can select music that offers both musical challenges and bolsters confidence. Unlike private community-based directors, elementary music teachers have the opportunity and advantage of experiencing multiple years with students before they reach an eligible grade for chorus membership. Since I teach kindergarten through 6th grade, I am able to project the kinds of repertoire future groups will be able to learn and perform.

Obviously it's easier to plan ahead when the population of the school maintains continuity year after year. Constantly shifting school clientele makes the selection of music a bit trickier. I'm fortunate to have taught in public schools with relatively limited migratory inclinations, thus making predictions for choral possibilities a bit easier. The process of selecting repertoire still takes an investment of time and energy, even when the musical and non-musical characteristics of potential members are somewhat familiar to the director.

Criteria to Consider When Selecting Repertoire

Beyond knowing your choristers and exercising criteria for their selection into the group, directors should establish and adhere to priorities when choosing music. Multiple directors, composers, and authors have provided guidelines to consider when choosing music for the children's chorus. Gackle suggested the literature selected should "provide the basis for musical experiences which teach, encourage, inspire, and create memories for life."[3] She suggested directors seek musical choices that:

---

[3] Lynne Gackle, "Selecting Choral Literature for Children's Choir, a Closer Look at the Process," *Choral Journal* 47, no. 5 (November 2006): 101.

- Facilitate vocal development
- Encourage musical development
- Utilize quality, age-appropriate texts
- Engage the mind and spirit of the singer
- Provide experiences with various styles, genres, languages, or cultures
- Entertain and engage the audience[4]

Bartle wrote, "A worthwhile piece will always help the child grow musically and help to develop the beauty of the child's voice."[5] She suggested directors consider music with the following questions in mind:

- Is the text worth learning?
- Does the selection have an interesting vocal line?
- Are the concepts of rhythm, harmony, counterpoint, and voice leading implemented in interesting ways?
- Is the shape and structure of the piece manageable for the chorus?
- Does the accompaniment add to the overall musicality of the vocal lines?
- Is the vocal range and tessitura set with children's voices in mind?[6]

---

[4] Ibid., 106.
[5] Bartle, *Sound Advice*, 182.
[6] Ibid.

In her book on teaching the elementary school chorus, Swears wrote:

> As you begin to select music for your chorus, be sure to ask, "Is this music worth learning? Does it have intrinsic value that will provide students with a worthwhile musical experience? Can the music be a building block to new musical learning? What are the possibilities for learning about tone color, diction, phrasing, harmony, melodic direction or rhythm?"[7]

Swears cautioned public school music teachers to consider the lyrics ("if it's not worth saying, it's not worth singing"), the range and tessitura, the melodic and harmonic lines, the level of difficulty, the accompaniment, and the suitability to the group:

> Will they enjoy learning and performing it? Will they feel a sense of pride and accomplishment presenting it to an audience? Does the overall character of the piece fit the needs of your group? Will you enjoy teaching and conducting it?[8]

Pagel and Spevacek recommended that choral directors select music based on one's teaching philosophy and long-term vision for the program. A balanced repertoire is suggested, one with educational benefits, enjoyment from the audience perspective, and accessibility to the singers. "You will certainly gain your students' respect and loyalty for respecting them enough to present a challenge."[9]

In my research of the instructional techniques of outstanding children's choir directors, the topic of selecting music was integral to the success of the programs observed. One director suggested that some music teachers were not aware of the abundance of music literature suitable for children's voices written by masters like Bach, Schumann, Holst, Bartók, or Copland. Sometimes, music teachers simply did not feel confident in the students' reaction or reception to music of the masters. She described reactions sometimes heard:

---

[7] Swears, 161.
[8] Ibid., 165.
[9] Randy Pagel and Linda Spevacek, *The Choral Director's Guide to Sanity...and Success!* (Dayton, OH: Heritage Music Press, 2004) 140.

They tell me "my kids would never like this." You're not going to let children say what math or science literature they want to learn and yet music teachers often let children decide what kind of musical literature they want to sing![10]

Another director noted:

One of the first things is that I have to like [the piece]. Number two is it has to say something that my students can relate to. Actually, it has to say something that I would like to say to them. It has to be so wonderful that I want to share it with them. This is a gift from me.[11]

Based on input from general music teachers who direct choirs within their public schools, my own experiences in selecting repertoire for a variety of choruses (my own groups, as well as regional and state honor choirs) and research conducted on the topic, my personal criterion for the musical choices I make for children's choral ensembles is as follows:

Repertoire Selection—Simple Criteria

- Consideration of the text: What words are sung? How are they set? Are they age-appropriate? If in a foreign language, do I have the necessary resources to teach the text with appropriate pronunciation?
- If the words are original (not based on existing poetry), do they have merit? Can they stand on their own, artistically?
- Will programming this selection provide harmonic variety? (Hearing all major-key pieces sung in unison is certainly not as interesting as mixed voicing and tonality.)
- Is the range and tessitura appropriate for my singers? Does it fit the age and particular group I'm directing? (This is particularly crucial if students as young as 3rd grade are included in the chorus.)
- Is the selection appropriate for the size of my ensemble? Will the number of students participating be able to sing the piece according to the composer's plan?
- What's the accompaniment like? How does it relate to and enhance the piece as a whole? Is some "enhancement" suggested, such as drums, a flute obbligato, a bass part, etc.?

---

[10] Bourne, "Instructional Techniques for Children's Choirs," 51.
[11] Ibid.

- There must an inherent value to the work. (It does not have to be high brow to be considered artistic, but will the piece showcase my group's strengths?)
- The pedagogical merits: What can I teach through the piece? More importantly, what can they learn?
- Level of challenge for my students: I don't want my singers stagnant. Introducing a piece that stretches them is appealing to us all, but I do want to be sure adequate rehearsal time is available to reach success and satisfaction with more challenging repertoire.
- Stylistic characteristics: Does the music fit specific stylistic qualities?
- The inherent beauty and appeal for the singers, director, and audience. It's really difficult to teach a piece I don't like or find little value in; likewise, selections should elicit some kind of response from singers and audience members.

Influences Affecting Repertoire Choices

The above criteria fall into major categories that influence the process of selecting music. These categories include:

- **Curricular influences:** How well a selection fits within the learning systems already in place for the general music educator as well as how well it expands the learning possibilities of those participating in chorus
- **Cultural influences:** Does the repertoire match and respect the culture and climate of the community?
- **Resource influences:** Is an accompanist available? What other support staff and mechanisms exist?
- **Audience influences:** Selections should be considered for their audience appeal and appreciation.

Curricular Influences

Within my current educational setting, students attend music class twice a week. They spend more time in the general music classroom than in choral rehearsal; therefore, the bulk of their music education occurs during their time in the music classroom. What is learned during the choral rehearsal is an extension and expansion of the music curricula all students (chorus members and non-chorus members) experience.

The music curricula is conceived of and dispensed through a philosophical framework that best reflects what is believed about instructional priorities. My own instructional priorities include the ability to apply skills necessary to sing in tune as well as the knowledge and understanding necessary to apply musical concepts.

Like many elementary general music educators, I teach curricular concepts through eclectic means. Within my music classroom, students sing, move, play instruments, create and improvise, learn to read melodic and rhythmic symbols, decode and analyze selections for their intent, form, and structure, and interpret how music relates to other cultures, time periods, and events.

Above and beyond conceptual information, my teaching philosophy promotes celebrating the spirit of the child while providing an environment rich in educational possibilities. The children I teach and direct in the choral ensemble are spirited individuals first, learners second, musicians/singers third, and chorus members fourth. As their general music teacher, I look for and select material, resources, and lessons that guide, motivate, and inspire. The students' goodwill and growth as successful citizens is my first priority.

As a music educator, my task is to teach in ways that lead to authentic and memorable learning experiences. Singing is one of the many skills exercised, honed, and prized within the general music curriculum. If I am doing the job effectively, singing is perceived as a positive experience by the children in my general music classes; as a result, they may choose to be a part of the chorus in 5th and 6th grade.

I choose to prioritize the organization and implementation of instruction with this hierarchy in mind—citizens first, students second, singers third, chorus members fourth. With this guiding system, the selection of choral music becomes an extension of my curriculum rather than a separate entity.

The music selected will hopefully elicit some kind of emotion, which in turn, makes that particular selection memorable, meaningful, and personally motivating. Pagel and Spevacek suggest the director ask herself, "Does the music you select make you and the chorus members feel sadness, joy, adoration, love, anger, silliness….something?"[12] I want the music selected to help students realize they are communicating a thought, a place, a condition, or a belief through the text and expression of the song.

---

[12] Pagel and Spevacek, 146.

For members of the choir, the repertoire selected should entice students to utilize their growing music vocabulary and skills. The relationship of what is learned in the general music class to what is applied through choral performance should overlap. For example, our chorus was learning Bernstein's "Gloria Tibi" (from the *Mass*) having recently listened to "Overture to *Candide*" (by the same composer) as part of a general music lesson. Several students immediately remembered the $\frac{7}{8}$ meter of the overture and related it to the $\frac{5}{8}$ setting of the choral number, summarizing that Bernstein must be a composer who loved odd-numbered meters.

Sometimes the song material used in the general music class will be programmed for the chorus, as a performance piece or warm-up selection. All chorus members learn the song in music class initially, but hearing it rehearsed and performed by 70 to 80 voices certainly enhances the experience for them.

The expectations for choral students are similar to what they experience in general music class: Choral students are expected to be learners during the rehearsal process. In order to incorporate curricular goals established for general music students in 5th and 6th grade, choral repertoire is selected to take that learning one step further. Students see, hear, and respond to the music differently when recognizable traits exist. They draw confidence from that which they know and are less hesitant to take steps toward new information. Answering the question, "What can students learn from this selection?" and coupling it with the answer to, "Why is this piece of value and merit for students to spend time learning?" links the academic and aesthetic merits for choosing certain works over others.

Marshall wrote: "All nine National Content Standards can be met through judicious selection and detailed preparation of elementary choral literature."[13] One can assume the standards might serve as instructional parameters when selecting repertoire, as the link between a varied program and inclusion of all nine standards is easily recognized. The National Standards in Music Education include:

1. Singing, alone and with others, a varied repertoire of music.
2. Performing on instruments, alone and with others, a varied repertoire of music.
3. Improvising melodies, variations, and accompaniments.
4. Composing and arranging music within specified guidelines.
5. Reading and notating music.
6. Listening to, analyzing, and describing music.
7. Evaluating music and music performances.
8. Understanding relationships between music, the other arts, and disciplines outside the arts.
9. Understanding music in relation to history and culture.[14]

Cultural Influences

Public school general music teachers are strongly advised to adhere to the guidelines and cultural protocol of the school environment. While laws and guidelines offer educational insight for programming sacred texts, for instance, there can be a covert level of acceptance within the larger school community. When teachers pay attention to societal norms existing within their school community, there is a sense of respect communicated throughout; parents and their children know that you have paid attention to their uniqueness and accept the cultural diversity and existent norms within the community.

---

[13] Herbert D. Marshall, "Elementary Choir Resources," *General Music Today* 18, no. 2 (2005): 38.

[14] From *National Standards for Arts Education.* © 1994 by Music Educators National Conference (MENC). Used by permission. The complete National Arts Standards and additional materials relating to the Standards are available from MENC—The National Association for Music Education, 1806 Robert Fulton Drive, Reston, VA 20191.

During the summer, I have the privilege of leading choral reading sessions for music teacher participants from multiple geographical areas of the country. The music selected represents a wide variety of genres, some of it quite sacred or centered around Christian messages (especially of the Christmas story). I normally ask the group of mostly public school music teachers how many of them can program choral selections with overt Christmas texts within their public school settings. Approximately half the participants raise their hands. The ones  who raise their hands often voice that their particular communities expect it. Conversely, those who do not raise their hands strongly voice the opposite—the community in their areas would find it inappropriate.

The National Association of Music Education (MENC) posted the following guidelines for programming pieces with possible issues for the community. The following questions are taken from the "Position Statement on the Use of Sacred Music in the Schools":

1. Was the music selected on the basis of its musical and educational value rather than its religious context?
2. Does the teaching of music with sacred text focus on musical and artistic considerations?
3. Are the traditions of different people shared and respected?
4. Is the role of sacred music one of neutrality, neither promoting nor inhibiting religious views?
5. Are all local and school policies on religious holidays and the use of sacred music observed?
6. Is the use of religious symbols or scenery avoided? Is performance in devotional settings avoided?
7. Is there sensitivity to the various religious beliefs represented by the students and parents?[15]

A rehearsal for a recent holiday concert for the Canyon Creek Chorus began with the singing of several pieces that mentioned Christmas traditions and references. Titles included "Christmas is Coming and We Are Getting Fat," "I'll

---

[15] The National Association for Music Education (MENC), "Music with a Sacred Text," http://www.menc.org/about/view/sacred-music-in-schools

Be Home for Christmas," and "Children, Go Where I Send Thee." By the third title, which referenced the "babe born in Bethlehem," one of my chorus members and the son of a rabbi said, "Mrs. Bourne! Come on!" I convinced him the remainder of the selections were mostly secular, non-holiday related, or in a foreign language. His reaction was honest and appreciated; it also helped me realize some kind of dialogue about the music selected would be a positive way to start the choral year.

Pagel and Spevacek wrote, "If directors take the time to select appropriate music and share even a small part of their decision-making process with the group, it will help secure buy-in from chorus members."[16] This has proven true time and time again.

Several years ago, we had several Jehovah's Witnesses in our community. The children were fantastic singers and quite interested in participating in chorus, but due to their religious beliefs they could not sing texts referencing holidays or patriotic themes. I did my best to program appropriately, and initiated communication with their parents to learn if participation in chorus was a feasible option for them.

Sharing the repertoire—titles and main body of the text—does require some effort, but doing so allows parents to discuss which songs are appropriate for their sons and daughters to sing and which are not. Those particular children did receive parental approval to be members of the chorus and were placed near the edge of the risers for a quiet departure when holiday or patriotic songs were performed. Likewise, they'd slip right back onto the risers when an approved selection occurred.

I do my best to select a varied program so that our audience feels comfortable listening to our selections. Understanding the community, learning the cultures represented in the school, and utilizing this knowledge when selecting repertoire is key. In addition, opening lines of communication with parents is exceedingly valuable, relevant, and important. While I do not allow others (like parents) to dictate what I choose, basic information of a cultural nature is appreciated and usually applied.

---

[16] Pagel and Spevacek, 144.

Resource Influences

No doubt, I am one lucky music teacher. For 26 of my 27 years as director of children's choirs, I have always found an accompanist. Someone always knew someone who knew someone who might know someone who could play piano! Our accompanists have had a myriad of backgrounds: local university students accompanying for independent study credit; high school seniors accompanying for senior-project credits; parent volunteers; former students who could handle a piece of medium difficulty while attending the junior high next door; and friends and neighbors who stepped in when the pickings were slim.

For the past several years, our accompanist at Canyon Creek has been the overload music teacher at our school. Her remarkable abilities as pianist have made possible a level of repertoire that would be out of reach with a less-skilled piano player. In fact, a few pieces were selected primarily because of her abilities. Prior to her, a superb pianist (parent volunteer) filled the role of accompanist for a record seven years in a row. She, too, was quite amazing in her roles as piano player and number-one fan of the chorus.

Having an accompanist is a priority for me as director. I'm capable of playing basic piano accompaniments and leading a group of singers with my head (in fact, this is normally how I lead singing in music programs when multiple classrooms are involved); however, fulfilling the role of both accompanist and director does not and will not work for me with a choral ensemble. I want the chorus to go above and beyond "singing together"; in order to pursue any degree of choral excellence, my hands and body must be free to help chorus members express the music. Gregoryk wrote, "An accompanist should be a priority for a public school chorus, leaving the director free to focus more completely on the choristers and choral sound."[17] (I used recorded accompaniment one season and found it to be personally restrictive and generally unappealing for me.)

Beyond the continuing position of accompanist, other resources appear from time to time that influence the choices made for repertoire. For instance, one student teacher was an oboe major, thus inspiring the selection of a choral piece that included oboe obbligato. Another time, one of our 6th-grade chorus members was taking jazz bass lessons, so a piece was chosen with a great walking bass line. Another student was

---

[17] Gregoryk, 30.

taking trap set lessons; consequently, a choral work was found
that had a good beginning-level drum set accompaniment.

The ethnic mix of our students provides multiple parents
and grandparents who speak non-English languages. Whether
the language is Spanish, Hawaiian, Chinese, Hindi, Hebrew,
or Portuguese, family members have served as wonderful resources for correct pronunciation and translation.

Final resource influencers are the directors at the middle
school/junior high and senior high. Each March, our school

group performs a concert with combined choirs. The evening ends with a massed spectacular that combines 250+ students from ages 10 to 18. The choir directors of the secondary schools and I search for repertoire that presents a musical challenge for all involved. The intent is to showcase each choir while combining voices to create a sense of singing continuity, from pre-adolescence to young adulthood. The event is always well received and the culminating number is a real show-stopper.

Audience Influences

Audiences should be considered when selecting music. On those occasions when my public school children's choirs performed for participants in state or regional music education conferences, music was selected that was a slight step beyond normal programming. I wanted the chorus to display the wide range of skills possible with 10- to 12-year-old public school children participating in a non-auditioned chorus. Music was selected that included marimba and drum ensemble, a parent soloist, multiple student instrumentalists, movement, sign language, foreign languages, etc. It was important to me that those particular audience members have a memorable experience, seeing and hearing something well beyond the typical school music program.

Although our performance for audiences of music educators were highlights for me, my students continue to be thrilled performing for their moms, dads, siblings, teachers, neighbors, and friends. The music performed for familiar folk should offer opportunities for audience members to think, "Wow, that piece was kind of hard!" "I didn't know kids could sing in other languages!" "Listen to that harmony—how unusual." "I know this one!" "This is so entertaining!"

Our student body serves as the audience for our December holiday concert, which is performed at school the week before break. I can always tell which song was the favorite, as I'll hear it on the playground later that day. Music selected should include a couple of tunes that are memorably entertaining, especially for an audience full of future chorus members!

Programming with Full Clientele in Mind

Based on the influences of curricula, culture, resources, and audience, how does a director narrow the selections to adequately program for a single performing season? When I narrow down selections, I want to be sure variety is evident.

Within a single program, my goal is to schedule selections that provide a mix of the following:

- Music with an interesting sound (due to the harmony, rhythm, tonality, changing moods, etc.)
- Music that is "jazzy" or in a straight-ahead jazz idiom (genre)
- Music representing places or times in the world (ethnic/world music or music of the Renaissance, Baroque, or Classical period)
- Music with text in a foreign language (especially if the text represents an existing culture within the school)
- Music that is recognizable by most audience members
- Music that offers the audience something to watch (a visual display through movement, an instrumental accompaniment, etc.)
- Music that provides the audience an opportunity to laugh
- Music that has solo sections
- Music that takes longer to learn due to the challenges it offers
- Music that links to events in or around the date of the performance (holidays, Music In Our Schools Month, etc.)

Frankly, I would find directing and teaching only one genre of music rather boring. It's important that my students experience diversity in the choral repertoire selected and taught as it reflects my overall belief in educating citizens of the world. If I believe the ensemble experience enhances the students' sense of community, expands their musical understanding, and creates a memorable experience for all involved, varied repertoire will be evident.

As director, I am the one who selects music based on multiple criteria driven by curricular, cultural, resource, and audience-appeal influences. It's up to me to choose pieces that teach, showcase the choir's strengths, and offer musical satisfaction as well as challenges. It's a time-consuming process, but well worth the effort.

The companion DVD captures portions of a performance given in December, 2007. The viewer will note singers performed songs *a cappella*, with drum ensemble accompaniment, with and without motion and movement, and with piano accompaniment. Further, a selection was included that was performed without me conducting. The variety offered provided the students with shifts in body position, facial expression, and feeling tone, and offered the audience opportunities to watch a host of visual stimulants as well as an opportunity to experience a wide range of emotion.

Repertoire Suggestions

I normally select music from a variety of publishers. Over the years, a few have emerged as favorites of mine. As publisher of some of the finest children's choral literature available, Heritage Music Press (HMP) is high on the list. The choral and general music editors at Heritage Music Press are invested in the choral and musical education of students and each year contribute excellent repertoire for consideration. Experience has taught me to look toward their selections first, as I know quality will be found.

I recommend the following titles as highly successful HMP compositions to use with children's choirs. Each was selected, rehearsed, and enthusiastically received by those who sang as well as those who listened. In some cases, the repertoire was selected for the Canyon Creek Chorus, while some were programmed for regional or all-state honor groups I was invited to guest conduct. I've included annotated comments on these particular titles for further information.

Additional HMP titles plus a list of my Top 20 titles from other publishers are listed in the Appendix, which begins on page 145. Each is highly recommended for its effectiveness with elementary level children's choruses or in cases where the younger ensemble has an opportunity to sing with an SATB choir.

Selected Octavo Repertoire: Heritage Music Press

A Jubilant Gloria
Mary Lynn Lightfoot (Two-part, 15/1795H)

An exciting work with meter shifts and dynamic and expressive changes. The form of the song is clear, offering a road map for students to follow and helping them to understand the structure of the piece. The text is in Latin; the accompaniment very supportive without playing the melodic line with the voices. A wonderful challenge for an older elementary chorus.

Calypso Noel
Linda Spevacek (Two-part, 15/1124H)

Set with typical Caribbean rhythms, this piece is scored for two-part chorus, piano, and miscellaneous small percussion. The form is very clear with verse/refrain, and the accompaniment is simple enough to be played by an advanced student pianist. Fun to sing, fun to listen to; a nice holiday-oriented addition.

Ching A Ring Chaw (and Great Gittin' Up Mornin')
arr. Linda Spevacek (Two-part, 15/1345H)

Years ago, I programmed Aaron Copland's "Ching-a-Ring Chaw" and enjoyed it immensely. I was delighted to introduce this particular arrangement to my students. Spevacek couples the "Ching a Ring Chaw" melody with "Great Gittin' Up Mornin'," thus reinforcing the concept of partner songs. The piano part is creative and enhances the melodies while relying on singers to carry the tunes.

Christmas Is Coming and We Are Getting Fat
Dave and Jean Perry (Two-part, 15/1627H)

The afternoon following our chorus performance of this selection, I heard this melody and words sung by younger students at recess and in the hallways of the school. It was an enormous hit with our audiences. The choir members found the words amusing and enjoyed choreographing movement that enhanced the comedic text. I appreciated the metric setting (a lively $\frac{6}{8}$ bounce to legato $\frac{4}{4}$), the ease in which harmony was created and sustained, and the ability for students to sing together without the director. (This piece can be heard in its entirety in the third chapter of the DVD).

Et In Terra Pax
Mary Lynn Lightfoot (Two-part, 15/2096H)

This piece was selected for the Oregon All-State Elementary Chorus. I wanted to experience the sound and exquisite musicality of this piece with extraordinary voices in a setting beyond the typical "mom and dad" audience base. The children and audience of music teachers loved this selection. As with all of Mary Lynn's compositions, it is packed with instructional possibilities. But the expressiveness of it rises well above its mechanical benefits.

Gloria
David Giardiniere (Two-part, 15/2200H)

Each year, I look for a selection that will challenge each singer in the ensemble. This piece certainly did that, while sustaining interest and focus throughout the instructional process. With its shifting meters, extended range of pitches, shifts in tonality, and Latin text, it keeps chorus members—and their director—thinking. The selection requires an accompanist who is well above average. (This selection may be heard in its entirety on the DVD).

Hope Is a Hidden Star
Mark Patterson (Two-part, 15/2385H)

This gorgeous selection includes a cello part that is key to the accompaniment. I invited one of our former chorus members, now a 10th-grade orchestra member, to perform with us. The message is full of hope, "Shining all around us, though we may not see its rays, hope will come again to light our way." A quality piece with an equally quality message.

Jingle All the Ways
Brad Printz (Two-part, 15/1651H)

This arrangement of "Jingle Bells" is very comical. It uses the text of the song and places it in a variety of rhythmic and melodically familiar melodies, including "Aura Lee," "The Blue Danube Waltz," and "The Stars and Stripes Forever." A very fun arrangement and a real challenge for upper elementary students.

Oh, Susanna
Stephen Foster, arr. Brad Printz (Two-part, 15/1194H)

A very fun yet challenging setting of this Foster tune. Tempos vary, as does the expressiveness of the piece. It is scored for piano and an ensemble of mixed small percussion. I've programmed this selection for my own chorus as well as regional groups with students with 200+ members. It's very doable and appealing to singers and audiences.

Peace Song (with "We Shall Overcome")
Greg Gilpin (Two-part, 15/2008H)

This selection was programmed for a Veteran's Day assembly at our school and was later used for an honor choir performance in another state. In both locations, it was well received and appreciated. The selection begins with a solo line, moving into a two-part section with the words, "So many people have helped shape our lives. Striving for truth, they have lived and died. We remember their faces, we remember their names..." The simplicity of "Peace Song" moves into a gorgeous setting of "We Shall Overcome" and ends with the simplicity of the opening solo. (A small portion of this selection can be heard on the DVD).

Pō La'i E
Linda Spevacek (Two-part, 15/1657H)

"Silent Night" sounds beautiful when sung in Hawaiian. I asked a parent, a native of Hawaii, to help with the pronunciation of the words, although Spevacek provides excellent guidelines. The melody of the familiar holiday carol combines with an original melody ("Peace Carol") to create a splendid harmonic blend resulting from the partner-song arrangement.

The Poet Sings
Z. Randall Stroope (SSA, 15/1376H)

This is a showcase number with welcome challenges throughout. It capitalizes on unison lines as well as three-part *divisi* sections near the end. The penultimate moment is the heterophonic setting of the words, "Stay the course, light a star, change the world where 'er you are." I've programmed this extraordinary piece for my own elementary chorus, regional groups, and all-state select choirs.

Zum Gali Gali
arr. Greg Gilpin (Two-part, 15/1824H)

This arrangement includes rhythmically spoken text and repeated phrases that make the piece very intriguing for singers and audience members. It is accompanied by drum and flute (this part can be played on recorder, as well). No piano accompaniment, which makes it a smart choice for directors without accompanists or desiring *a cappella* numbers.

Favorite Resources

With the intent to program varied repertoire, where and how does the search begin? There are multiple paths to take. Music retailers offer opportunities to read through stacks of new octavos at choral reading workshops held throughout the country. In addition, many offer e-clubs, supplying monthly updates of new music to subscribers.

Beyond music retailers, I often search for music selected for regional and all-state choruses. The research begins by surveying the state music education Web sites that are known for offering elementary all-state choirs. Often, I will look at the repertoire lists of children's choruses performing at regional and national conferences of MENC (The National Association of Music Education; www.menc.org), ACDA (American Choral Directors Association; www.acdaonline.org) and AOSA (American Orff-Schulwerk Association; www.aosa.org).

When attending music conferences, I peruse the exhibition booths of retailers and publishers. It's always a thrill to actually meet a recognized composer at the booths. Often, reading sessions will be offered at state, regional, and national conferences that feature familiar names in the children's choral idiom.

The Web site www.choralnet.org provides a place to dialogue and ask questions of other directors as well as search comments on repertoire selection and programming for a specific occasion, voicing, etc. For example, if the children's choir does not have an accompanist, one might seek information on *a cappella* selections that work within the child's vocal tessitura.

As mentioned above, I will look at the list of choral octavos within a single publishing company. Most major publishers maintain updated Web sites that provide descriptions of titles as well as available voicings. In recent years, recordings of audio clips or entire songs are accessible through many publishers' Web sites.

Primary sources consulted for this book (and listed in the bibliography) include suggested repertoire that's still available for purchase. Texts by Bartle, McRae, Pagel and Spevacek, Rao, Stultz, and Swears list suggested repertoire for primary choirs through junior high students. These authors can be trusted to offer pieces that work for a variety of children's choral ensembles. In addition, Marshall's articles in *General Music Today* include suggested titles with specific information offered for each selection.

Finally, I've learned of multiple titles through recordings of professional children's choirs. There are several ensembles within the United States (as well as in my area of Seattle, Washington) that record and market CDs annually and use the proceeds to help their groups' financial commitments. I highly recommend seeking the recordings of these superb groups. (A simple Google search for "recordings of professional children's choirs" provides ample information.)

Budget Basics

Purchasing choral music does cost money. Those on a fixed budget might find stocking the choral library to be a long, extended process. Our school normally receives some funds from the district office. Each year, I take part of that money and purchase a couple of new selections. A classroom set is housed in a file cabinet sitting in my music room.

While our choral library grows year after year, I do explore other options. Directors can make dollars stretch by purchasing bound copies of multiple songs. Heritage Music Press, for example, offers several in multiple voicings (see list beginning on page 146). Mary Lynn Lightfoot, Choral Editor of Heritage Music Press, indicated that several publishers are "keenly aware of the budgetary restrictions" so offer collections at a reduced rate compared to the purchase of individual octavos. These are not reproducible, however HMP and other notable publishers do include songs suitable for young choirs in collections that allow the buyer to reproduce whatever amount is needed. Quality recorded accompaniment CDs are available for both the compilations (separate purchase) and collections (included with the book).

Directors might want to take opportunities to arrange music for their students, provided they are appropriate and in the public domain. I've also invited exceptional students to assist in arrangements with marimba or drum ensembles.

Many districts maintain a central library of scores, which may be checked out by employees.

Two other possibilities: choral directors can pursue the purchase of music through curriculum textbook monies; after all, the octavos are the "text" for a chorus. Finally, parent organizations can be extremely active in their fundraising and tax-exempt contributions. Within our PTA budget, we have a budgeted line-item called "music enhancement." The monies within this fund have provided the chorus with several quality selections of music.

Bartle wrote:

> Finding adequate funds to purchase music and supplies seems to be a persistent problem. While music is costly and a budget is necessary, I do feel that financial constraints cannot be blamed for all our ills. Some of the finest work I have seen was done by conductors who did not have adequate budgets.[18]

Bartle suggested fund raising for the specific purpose of purchasing music as well as approaching administrators and parents for financial support to that end. She also promotes

---

[18] Bartle, *Sound Advice*, 89.

scrounging: "Find schools that are closing, teachers who are retiring, publishing companies that are merging and have clearance sales, and churches that are amalgamating and discarding music no one uses anymore."[19]

If the chorus is valued as part of an extensive offering within the public school, expanded choral repertoire should be funded. Teachers are encouraged to investigate creative ways to support the composers, distributors, and publishers who have learned what we've known all along—our kids are worth it.

Selecting the music the children's chorus sings isn't an easy or fast process. Time to search is a reality: Nothing replaces this process. If the chorus is to be conceived of and received as an ensemble with high standards of performance, the music heard must be above and beyond what might be more appropriately used in the general music classroom.

The repertoire chosen is a reflection of the director's belief in the capacity of her singers. Since a public school children's chorus has the potential to reach heightened musical abilities, it truly is the director who establishes the "what" before the "how." Great music, well taught, inspires. It's worth the extra effort to provide excellent repertoire, appropriately selected, for our elementary students.

[19] Ibid.

Rehearsal and Management Strategies

Let's pause to review the process for establishing a children's choir within the elementary school. More often than not, the ensemble is organized and directed by the school's general music teacher, who offers the ensemble as part of or as an extension to her position as the school's general music teacher. Support is gained through conversations with the building administrators and other educators in the building. Criterion is determined for identifying and recruiting choir members; repertoire is selected based on the overall goals, aspirations, and abilities for the group. A rehearsal time frame and venue is identified and scheduled. It's time to get started!

As with any other topic guiding the established elementary school children's choir experience, process guides purpose, form follows function. That's certainly true for rehearsal organization and management. The director will find that predetermining processes and systems for rehearsals will help the group make steady progress. In order to function at their best, students need a director who will invest critical preparation time and thought before rehearsals begin.

Elementary music teachers are accustomed to the organizational requirements that come with managing large groups. When classrooms are pooled together for typical public performances, a teacher may have 100+ students to work with at the same time. Teachers quickly become experts at communicating a schedule, an agenda, and an overview of necessary steps for a successful program to occur. They understand that sequential instruction leads to desired results. They become masters at breaking lessons into small parts, knowing that each lesson leads to a bigger picture. These skills are necessary for success within the general music teacher's job and are extremely essential for success as chorus director.

Above and beyond the ability to teach and transmit information, however, is the capacity to transform and motivate a group of public school kids to become a choral ensemble. The general music teacher who strives to have an excellent children's choir within her school must establish and teach rehearsal and performance protocol. A successful director must possess an organizational sense that makes the most of limited rehearsal time.

The elementary choral director needs the personal skills necessary to convince her singers that choir is something unique and artistic, deserving of membership and regular attendance. Boonshaft wrote that music teachers must teach students "why they need to care, what they need to listen for... and how their efforts...make all the difference."[1]

> We simply need to have our enthusiasm, intensity, work ethic, sense of urgency, excitement, focus, energy, high expectations and willingness to show extremes of emotion; [these become] contagious.[2]

Rehearsing a public school children's choir taps into, and extends, the energy supply and attention level of the busy general music teacher. Knowing the physical effort exerted in fulfilling the elementary classroom music role, it's essential that chorus rehearsals are well planned in advance to keep the ensemble productive and positive, as well as to maintain the health of the director.

Walking into rehearsal and winging it is not fair to the students and will eventually cause them to lose momentum and interest. Pagel and Spevacek wrote, "The students are a reflection of the teacher, plain and simple. If you are enthusiastic about your job, your students will be enthusiastic about their learning."[3] Likewise, if the teacher/director demonstrates respect for her student's time and effort by having things in place before rehearsals begin, everyone wins. With preparatory steps based on the "where, what, how, who, and why" inquiry method, chances are rehearsals will be effective, efficient, and excellent for all involved.

---

[1] Peter Boonshaft, *Teaching Music with Passion: Conducting, Rehearsing, and Inspiring* (Galesville, MD: Meredith Music Publications, 2002) 175.
[2] Ibid.
[3] Pagel and Spevacek, 9.

Before Rehearsal Begins

Prepare the Rehearsal Venue

Once the rehearsal time frame and venue are selected (the "where"), steps need to be taken to be sure nothing short of an earthquake interrupts that schedule. Since I use a classroom other than my own (the gymnasium), it is critical for me to formally reserve it each time it's used for afterschool rehearsals or evening concerts.

In many schools and districts, any function occurring outside of the school day must be reserved on a master schedule. By formally reserving our gymnasium each Wednesday from 3:00–4:30 I shouldn't have chorus interrupted by some unforeseen community event. (When I forgot to reserve it, recreational basketball players showed up at 4:10 ready to take the court; their group had reserved the gym through the master calendar the district maintains.)

Getting the venue settled is a major first step. The choral director should also be sure to communicate with the custodian (who locks rooms and doors when the day is done), the office personnel (who field phone calls when a panicked chorus parent forgets it's Wednesday and wonders why his or her child did not get off the bus), and any colleague who teaches in the rehearsal area (since we use our gym, our PE teacher was the first one I consulted when Wednesday after school was selected).

Many choral directors use their own music classrooms. While I have used the music room for rehearsals, it is not an ideal location for a group with 80 or more singers. Our gym has built-in steps leading up to a stage. This provides natural risers for us to use. In addition, the gym is good-sized, allowing adequate space for the kids to blow off a bit of energy while transitioning from their regular day to the choral rehearsal.

The director anticipates what materials and conditions must be in place before the kids enter the rehearsal venue. In my particular situation, everything is transported from the music room to the gym stage during lunch—the box of music folders, the piano bench, music stands, any visual or material tools to be used, the rehearsal plan (written on a big piece of construction paper). The piano is rolled in as the students arrive for rehearsal (as it is used in the afternoon for general music classes so can't be moved during lunch).

My lunchtime routine is always the same on rehearsal days. I make sure the sound system and microphone are working. If the basketball goal is not being used that afternoon, I'll activate the mechanical system to pull the goal upward to the ceiling. Although students stand during a majority of our rehearsal, they sometimes sit on the built-in steps. I'll look at the steps' current condition and will not hesitate to pull out a broom if they are seeped with sand and mud. (On chorus days, I'm sure to bring a "one-handed lunch"—a lunch I can eat with one hand while the other hand takes care of pre-rehearsal business!)

Director Responsibilities

Several authors have specific recommendations offered to help directors prepare for and execute the ideal rehearsal. Bartle suggested the director consider both "musical and mechanical" preparatory steps.[4] She emphasized the need to establish and implement routines, methods, and cues for "getting control" at the beginning of the rehearsal, and establishing "realistic expectations" for what can be accomplished within the rehearsal time frame.[5]

Rottsolk listed key responsibilities of the director before the first rehearsal commences:

- Choose music carefully and well
- Know the score

---

[4] Bartle, *Sound Advice*, 59.
[5] Ibid., 63.

- Search constantly and intently for the intention of the composer
- Develop an informed concept of musical style—know what you want to hear
- Practice conducting gesture that communicates wordlessly, expressively, and efficiently
- Know what you want to accomplish
- Plan to establish correct pitch, rhythm, tempo, intonation, dynamics, balances, articulation, and languages
- Find potential trouble spots and prepare lessons to introduce and teach[6]

Bartle provided a checklist for preplanning what she calls the "ideal" rehearsal:

- Begin and end on time
- Post a well-planned list of pieces to work on and activities for all to see
- Implement appropriate warm-ups not only geared to voices but also to skills related to pieces being rehearsed
- Start with pieces that are familiar
- Teach skills that improve musical knowledge
- Keep talking from the director to a minimum
- Interject humor
- Give children the feeling of satisfaction, enjoyment, accomplishment, and importance[7]

Bartle added, "An excellent rehearsal is perhaps an art form in itself. Conducting a rehearsal requires total concentration and the complete integration of body, mind, and spirit."[8] The director's preparedness is ultimately the key to success.

Finally, McRae emphasized the need to plan and to know the music first and foremost. She suggested, "Most directors would be wise to anticipate what exercises might be appropriate for the vocal and musical requirements of the piece at hand."[9] In addition, McRae described the need to develop

---

[6] Rebecca Rottsolk, "Rehearsal Techniques: The Responsibility of the Conductor" (paper presented at the American Choral Directors Association Inservice, Seattle, WA, October 2003) 1.

[7] Bartle, *Sound Advice*, 37.

[8] Ibid., 33.

[9] McRae, 155.

verbal and nonverbal communication skills, to practice conducting expressively and meaningfully, and to predispose what
management systems will help.

> A variety of conditions must be present for the rehearsal to
> flow from one activity to the next…The management of a
> successful rehearsal depends upon all the conditions in the
> environment that affect morale and learning.[10]

Establish Routines, Habits, and Systems

Regardless of rehearsal venue, key preparatory steps before
rehearsals commence lead to efficiency once students arrive.
In addition to venue selection, basic systems of organization
need to be established (the "what" and "how"). These systems include decisions as to what students do once they enter
the rehearsal venue, where they put backpacks and coats (if
before or after school), what cues are used to officially begin
rehearsal, where they stand or sit, how they get their music,
and what they can expect to occur within the rehearsal time
frame. So much of effective rehearsal protocol boils down to
consistent routines and habits predetermined and taught by
an organized director.

---

[10] Ibid., 161.

As educators will attest, children develop confidence when routines exist. They learn more efficiently and productively when habits are established. With a once-a-week rehearsal, I want to make every minute count. If students know and understand what routines exist, why they exist, and how they are to participate within them, we can begin rehearsal with a sense of purpose and preparedness. Through experience, I've learned to teach routines and habits at the first rehearsal and reinforce them throughout the season.

As director, I must project what needs to occur in order to help me be at my best. This is particularly vital since I teach a full day prior to the rehearsal. When students arrive at chorus rehearsal, I'm also arriving. Not ideal, but a reality in my particular public school setting. Systems are in place that allow the students to make the shift from their classroom setting to the rehearsal setting, knowing that events have been preplanned and prepared to meet their basic needs.

When students arrive in the gym after school, they understand that the piano will be rolled in, the sound system rolled out, the box of choral folders retrieved from the stage and set on the floor, the music stands put in place, and the bench retrieved and placed in front of the piano. They know to help our PE teacher put away any mats or hanging ropes or to retrieve equipment he might need assistance with. They know the short period of time between class and chorus time needs to be used for afterschool snacks, getting to the bathroom, socializing with friends, returning any paperwork to me, etc.

Beyond the mechanical and managerial parts of the job, it is my responsibility to know and anticipate what the chorus members will experience from the beginning of rehearsal to the end. I must have an image of what particular parts of the rehearsal will look like, sound like, and feel like. These need to be communicated honestly and directly so that students can perform at their best. Anticipating in advance what the students (and director) should look like and sound like guides instruction supports the learning environment, promotes confidence to all involved.[11]

With thought, anticipation, effort, and time, the director's routines and habits pay off. The chorus members learn what they can expect from the director, and, in turn, what the director should be able to expect of them.

---

[11] Bourne, Patricia A., *Inside the Music Classroom* (Dayton, OH: Heritage Music Press, 2007).

Rehearsal Etiquette and Responsibility

Communicate Expectations

During our first rehearsal, students sit on the floor of the gym where they are welcomed. Students are introduced to our accompanist (if unknown to the chorus members), statistical information is provided (number of 5th graders, number of 6th graders, number of second-year chorus members, etc.), and overall expectations are revealed. These expectations are divided into two sections: What students can expect from me, as director of the group, and what I, as director, will expect from each and every chorus member.

Communicated in terms of what chorus members see, hear, and experience, these expectations outline what will occur during our time together. They outline systems that affect director and student responsibilities as well as frame the behavioral and musical etiquette displayed at rehearsals.

What students can expect of the director

1. There will be a lesson plan for each and every rehearsal. It will be written and posted for all students to see.
2. Music has been selected and prepared for instruction. It is organized and ready for student use.
3. Rehearsal materials and resources are ready for use
4. The director will speak directly and informatively
5. High standards of musicianship will be the norm
6. Honest assessment of what is heard and seen will be communicated
7. The director has a deep belief that the choral experience should be above and beyond what is experienced in general music, with instructional systems in place to prove that
8. Some kind of systematic communication with parents will be established
9. Trust and faith in members of the chorus will be consistent; the director will see every member of the group as a highly capable musician who is choosing to be a part of an artistic ensemble
10. Rehearsals will be full, preplanned, and organized to help students improve each and every time

What the director expects of chorus members

1. Use best vocal technique and consistently use habits that help singing improve
2. Treat each other and the director with respect and kindness
3. Show support for the chorus by telling others you are proud to be a member of the group
4. Help students in the chorus who need assistance
5. Know when to talk and when not to talk; exercise self-discipline
6. Keep track of paperwork and turn things in on time (permission forms, parent volunteer sheets, etc.)
7. Treat music and folders with care
8. Offer to help the director with set-up and tear-down chores
9. Congratulate soloists, thank accompanist often, support peer leaders
10. Do something obvious each and every rehearsal to individually improve and to help the group improve

Stating expectations is a beginning: Reinforcing them each and every rehearsal takes tremendous commitment. I highly recommend selecting expectations that are worth supporting on a consistent basis. As chorus members learn the director means what she says and says what she means, progress will be made.

Gumm wrote "What you put into your teaching is what you get back....If you predict artistry, think and communicate artistry, you get it to the fullest ability of your students."[12] On the other hand, if the general music teacher/children's choir director sees her students as "just kids" and accepts minimum effort from them (and herself), students are stuck with those results. Establishing rules of conduct and effort is crucial for student achievement. I really like a quote from Pagel and Spevacek:

> The only way for students to gain achievement is through the leadership of the teacher, *not the other way around.*[13]

During the Rehearsal: Creating a Learning Environment

Successful rehearsals provide opportunities for students to recognize their improvement, celebrate achievements, become acquainted with new material, build on skills and knowledge, expand vocabulary and vocal technique, assume leadership roles, provide input and evaluative statements, engage in listening and movement activities, and make connections between repertoire and life. In short, the rehearsal is established as an environment where profound learning can occur.

Learning occurs when students understand what to do. Since I leave very little room for confusion, I teach chorus members the following:

- How to enter the rehearsal venue
- What to do once they are in
- When to shift from before-rehearsal free time to rehearsal mode
- Where to stand or sit
- How to get the music from its storage place and into their hands
- Where to place their eyes and what to do during warm-ups
- How to get the director's attention appropriately
- Why certain physical and mental processes must be engaged to warm-up or review old material or learn new vocal techniques

---

[12] Gumm, 151.
[13] Pagel and Spevacek, 7.

With adequate preparation, the chorus rehearsal progresses like a finely tuned lesson plan. There are activities to get students ready for information, materials on hand for them to review and learn, opportunities to evaluate themselves and be evaluated (by the director), and insight as to what the next steps are in the process.

Lesson Planning 101: Warm-ups to Closers

Chorus members are electing to spend their time in rehearsal. It's up to the director to make that time as meaningful as it can be. Achievement and progress must be obvious to the students. Helping them understand that a steady, intent progression will occur—rehearsal to rehearsal—creates trust and faith that success will be reached and that their director knows what she is doing.

When I select repertoire for my elementary school chorus, I do so with instructional sequencing in mind. There will be selections that come together quickly and others that require short periods of concentrated time over several weeks. There will be pieces that need prerequisite skills in place to fully achieve the composer's intent, for both the students and director. Some pieces will present a challenge and may require the director to do more convincing, while others are easily taught due to their clarity, immediate appeal, and learning ease.

Regardless of repertoire, lesson planning that makes sense to the director and to the chorus members must be established. Most directors begin rehearsal with warm-ups. Students won't necessarily understand why this stage is included in each rehearsal unless it's explained. It's easy for students to see warm-ups as separate from the necessary order of business—learning the music!

Most vocal warm-ups should be attached to that which is learned over the course of the rehearsal. Physical warm-ups are also helpful, especially if the students are entering with no time to stretch or engage in physical activity. Since my students have opportunities to play in the five to ten minutes between sedentary classroom time and rehearsal, their bodies are usually running at a high energy level. Warm-ups for us become an opportunity to focus, to think, to feel the sensation of productive air support.

Goetze suggested that warm-ups should be structured around general skills or specific problems in the music to be rehearsed. Isolating the rhythmic, melodic and harmonic challenges of selections will streamline the proficiency and efficiency for learning. Goetze also recommended that music reading skills be incorporated into warm-up routines. Students can follow patterns drawn from repertory and answer questions like:

- Which notated pattern matches the one I'm singing?
- On which note did I stop?
- How did I change the melody you see? (or, find my error)
- Name this notated (and known) tune without hearing it first[14]

When I write the lesson plan for the week, I start with the music we will rehearse. Once that's solidified, I'll write warm-ups to help support what will be reviewed or learned. For instance, one selection we're currently working on has a series of words with two vowel sounds (dipthongs). In our warm-ups, we'll sing a series of scales ending in a word with the dipthong:

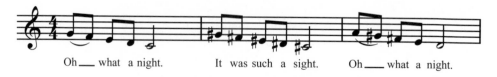

If a particular text has multiple ending consonants that present a challenge, those words will be used in warm-up passages. One such example follows. It is based on text heard in "Christmas is Coming and We are Getting Fat," and may be viewed on DVD.

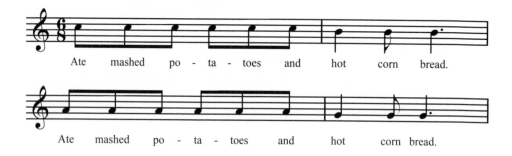

---

[14] Mary Goetze, "The Children's Choir: An Ideal Setting for a Musical Education" (paper presented at the Washington Music Educators Conference, Yakima, Washington, February 2008).

A final example relates to selections that offer some unique metric twists. If I want students to feel complex and changing meters, I'll include warm-ups that not only emphasize how a meter is counted, but also work on the vowels and consonants apparent when singing numbers.

Warm-ups that stretch the vocal bands and ligaments are very helpful when the upper range of the children's voices will be engaged. The singers start with an "oo" vowel and glissando as high as they can, with careful attention to not strain, not raise the chin, not change the shape of the vowel, and with a forward head tone present. At their highest point, they begin a gradual glissando lower, going as low as they can with the "oo" vowel in a light registration. (This particular warm-up is demonstrated on the DVD.)

During our one hour and 15 minute rehearsal, warm-ups last around 10 minutes, give or take a few. If they have worked effectively, the students' bodies, minds, and spirits are ready for the next wave of rehearsal sequence.

Plenty of time during the first and second rehearsals is provided to teach protocol and routines. Beyond those goals, I will normally include multiple opportunities for singers to demonstrate their skills in interpreting conducting gesture, display what participation looks like and sounds like in chorus rehearsal, show how to focus their eyes to follow the music, and become familiar with the pacing and expectations of members.

Yes, we do sing! Normally, we will tackle a couple of selections that are easily read. Songs that are unison or have a clear, repetitive form, or those with some semblance of familiarity will be introduced during the first rehearsals. I want students to feel success on day one. I want them walking out singing one of the chorus songs that was introduced.

By the third or fourth rehearsal, the students have looked at and listened to each song in the folder. The "middle stretch"—rehearsals three through nine—is when the music moves from "I barely know it" to "this part is familiar" to "I know the text and notes" to "It's close to performance level." Students should be included in the process of diagnosing how to improve. During the middle stretch of rehearsals, I'll ask students to evaluate their individual progress and to provide input on what it will take to improve.

The DVD includes footage taken from two middle-stretch rehearsals, #3 (October 3) and #8 (November 7). In each rehearsal, warm-ups drawn from challenges within particular selections were included. Beyond that, songs were practiced with increasing specificity from October to November. The following describes the rehearsal plans for each:

Rehearsal #3 (October 3)
- Warm-ups: attention to vowels, "ah" to "ee," intervals to follow opening melody of "Hava Na Shira"
- Introduce "Hava Na Shira" (6th-grade learned in general music)
- "Find the spot" in octavo of "Christmas is Coming and We are Getting Fat" (legato section? Where does the round start? Where does *subito p* occur?, etc.)
- Lift and bounce with shifting meter of "Gloria." Listen to recording. Follow form of the piece with kids holding cards representing sections.
- Orientation of "Gloria" octavo: Start and stop; "Where did we stop?" measure number and section. Speak words for clarity of Latin pronunciation. Review A sections, isolate B section (page 4, part 2, in d minor). Attention to B natural in A section, measure 37. Attention to shift from minor to major key in final A section.
- Review sections known, "Watu Wote"
- End with recap of "Hava Na Shira"

Rehearsal #8 (November 7)
- Warm-ups: include stretching (students were sitting through a long assembly in the afternoon). Attention to breath and pacing of exhale
- Warm-ups: descending scale (C major) using § meter and singing words, "Ate mashed potatoes and hot corn bread." Ascending scale includes word "biscuits of Grandma's fame." Attention to crisp consonants

- Start at legato section of "Christmas Is Coming." Clarity of words, even though it's legato. Review whole song, overt actions and expression of words clear. Develop ability to sense cut-offs, entrances
- Select witness to watch chorus sing "Christmas Is Coming"; identify students showing the words "what I see"
- Vocabulary links: legato, round, fermata, meter shift
- "Hava Na Shira": Show solfége; students identify which of the three sections matches what they see shown using hand signals
- "Ayelevi": Use new drumming ensemble. Run form (call-response, then drumming ensemble, then call-response with ensemble)
- "Gloria": Emphasis on tonality (minor vs. major) and meter ($\frac{6}{8}$ vs. $\frac{3}{4}$). Review pronunciation of Latin. Introduce Coda (starts like the B section, but then what happens?)
- Other selections rehearsed according to remaining time
- Self evaluate chorus on each selection with following scale:

1. Not a bit ready to perform
2. We can sing it through, but not very well
3. We're moving forward, making good progress on this one
4. We're sounding good—we're confident on this one
5. This selection is ready to perform for an audience

By rehearsals ten, eleven, and twelve—the "big-push stretch"—we are rehearsing what performance looks like and sounds like, as opposed to what rehearsal looks like and sounds like. Anything I want to see and hear during the performance must be built in to these final rehearsals. The lesson plan is simple: "Run program."

By our first performance, music is memorized, students know what to expect at each and every venue; they have reached a level of proficiency that helps them feel proud of their accomplishments. Through strategically planned rehearsals, they have bonded as a community and have developed assurance that each person in the group knows what to do, when to do it, how to do it, and why it's to be done that way.

Rehearsal routines and well-planned lessons are essential to success, regardless of the size and intent of the elementary chorus. Students are flexible and will adhere to the behavioral and musical expectations set by the director. In turn, the director has taken the time to prepare the venue as well as the materials and resources needed for rehearsal. She has included opportunities for students to laugh together, to express opinions openly, to evaluate their improvements and achievements, and to celebrate and enjoy each individual's contribution to the community.

Above and beyond that, the teacher *knows the music*—she has played through it, sung through it, considered the unique aspects of each selection, and drawn conclusions as to the sequence of instructional strategies to lead toward success in performance. She has practiced conducting each selection so that singers might draw from her gesture the appropriate feel for each piece. The desired sound of each piece is apparent to the director long before students begin the rehearsal process. She is able to anticipate trouble spots and address those through various techniques. The music has the capacity to come alive due to her study and efforts.

Conducting 101

Like many musicians, I enjoy watching what a director does to bring about certain sounds with his or her ensemble. Some directors make the simplest of motions and yield unbelievable results (Weston Noble, for instance—the man would barely move and his choirs would sing with a robust, powerful, musical tone or with the quietest and gentlest of sounds). I recommend that the director of an elementary children's choir use gestures that, 1) best help the students achieve the level of musicianship they are capable of and, 2) do not interfere with the visual image of children singing together.

I have three overriding guidelines regarding conducting:

1. Make motions that reflect the motion and expression of the music, not just the beat
2. Do as little as possible so that the audience can focus on the singers
3. Connect with chorus members via facial expression and eyes. They should be able to tell what piece you are conducting by looking at the gesture, the face, the eyes, and the body position.

Bartle commented:

The bottom line must be that anything a conductor can do to help the performance be convincing and artistic should be done, as long as the conductor is using [clear] patterns and the gestures don't detract from the music... Every single gesture should be meaningful if you wish to perform the work with consummate artistry.[15]

Bartle advised that directors must be "concerned about interpreting the music for the choir and not impressing the audience. Your aim is to help the singers have confidence."[16] When I taught at the university level, many student teachers were observed in rehearsal and performance settings. It was essential to reel in any and all conducting antics that drew attention to themselves rather than the students. They needed to be reminded that the majority of the audience was there to see a student, not watch the gyrations of a student teacher!

I've also watched directors who clearly rely on following the score during performance. It's hard to imagine conducting a group without eye contact: I rely on non-verbal glances to show approval for a phrase beautifully sung and to call attention to more breath support or focused tone. Using my

---

[15] Bartle, *Lifeline For Children's Choir Directors*, 33.
[16] Ibid., 32.

eyes, as well as my ears, I can fix problems with intonation by adjusting the shape of a child's mouth or gesturing tall vowels and expressive faces.

Keeping one's face in the score does not mix with kids. It's essential to look at the singers, particularly those in the elementary grades. To help guide my eyes while conducting, I prepare the score; the marks help me emphasize particular sections of the music and assist in organizing instruction of the piece. Understanding the schema of the entire piece, and knowing what I want the piece to sound like before teaching it to the kids, is vital.

Bartle mentioned:

> It cannot be stated often enough that before the first rehearsal begins the conductor must do a thorough analysis of the piece and have a complete understanding of it. The conductor needs to begin, as it were, with the end in mind and needs to hear the ideal performance of the work in his or her own inner ear. All further preparation and rehearsals will be organized with this ideal performance in mind.... Conducting is far more than setting the correct tempo and keeping the piece together.[17]

Any symbols or notes to myself are added before the selection is rehearsed, as the selection is rehearsed, and when it is ready for performance. I want to remember what I did that helped the students and will make notes on the score to that effect. This is simple score preparation. As an example, my marked copy of "Gloria" is provided at the end of this chapter. This selection is also included in the rehearsal and performance sections of the DVD, allowing connections to be made between the visual and aural.

When considering the addition of a choral ensemble to an already full-time schedule, it's easy to wonder whether it's worth it. The time, the effort, the planning, the set-up, the communication, and the energy consumed to establish and maintain a highly functioning elementary chorus can be overwhelming. Why do it?

---

[17] Ibid., 43.

It's the kids. They deserve it. They are the ones who will look back on their time in the elementary chorus with full knowledge that it was positive, packed, and perceived as something special. As Boonshaft put it:

[Within our students] we see unlimited potential. We see in them what others, even they, can't see....Simply put, we envision what our students can become and then we work to make it happen. We see what's possible, and then teach until we set them free to be what they can be....It doesn't matter whether our students move in giant steps or baby steps, take to it naturally or with great effort. We take them from where they are—how they are—and gently help them try to touch the stars....We allow them to grow and develop as feeling, caring people, and in so doing help mold the future for generations we will never see.[18]

Directors of elementary choral ensembles have one of the best opportunities to provide a glimpse of the power of music. Preparing quality repertoire to be performed artistically requires hard work, commitment, a sense of responsibility and service to others, follow-through, determination, and willingness to reach beyond what might be considered the norm. Think of the many ways our students benefit!

---

[18] Boonshaft, 231–232.

Gloria
Two-part Chorus and Piano*

Traditional Latin — explain what this means

David Giardiniere

Ranges: Part I   Part II

-INTRO-   explain 63/84 meaning

Forging ahead ♩. = 96 (♪ = ♪ throughout)

Sets the mood!

very separate

"Glaw"

Ⓐ

unison

Glo-ri-a in ex-cel - sis, glo-ri-a in ex-cel - sis,

Glo-ri-a in ex-cel - sis, glo-ri-a in ex-cel - sis,

d minor

C   B♭

Duration: approx. 2:30
*Also available for SATB (15/2199H).

15/2200H-3

⭐ *left hand different;*
sets up next section

Purposeful
Performances

Like the lengthy chain of events for establishing and sustaining a high functioning elementary chorus, successful and purposeful performances reflect those steps taken in thorough preparation. Performances are the reward for the time, energy, and focus invested by all constituents in a choral ensemble. Student members can proudly stand before an audience and showcase their musicianship while parents reap the joy of watching their children demonstrate poise and professionalism. The director is able to recognize the results and evidence of her leadership in authentic, real-life settings. "Performance opportunities are critical."[1] They mark the culmination of time well spent.

[1] Bartle, *Sound Advice*, 73.

By the time performances occur, the chorus is as ready as it can be. The level of skills demonstrated is a reflection of what has occurred in the week-to-week practice sessions. Experienced directors know that being ready is so much more than having the notes and words of the music memorized. In order for performances to be memorable, pleasurable, and dynamic learning experiences for chorus members, the director must take the time to consider the non-musical facets of performance etiquette.

Performance: Non-Musical Necessities

A chorus with high standards of achievement will display a level of commitment to each other and to the ensemble that is evident in how they dress, how they behave, and how organized they are before, during, and after each performance. Most audiences are exceedingly aware of the difference between a group of kids who come together for a single performance with casual attire (albeit an equally casual attitude) and those choirs that have a professional appearance and demeanor. Ultimately, the visual image of a chorus that dresses in some kind of similar concert attire, whose members know how to behave in public, and who know what to do in performance situations reflects on the director.

Pagel and Spevacek noted:

> Directors have the greatest influence on how the stage is set, how the music is prepared, and how the students are guided to perform in public, not to mention how prepared they are as individuals to make it all happen in a performance. Students will dress the way you tell them to….If they are told not to talk on the risers, they won't. If the music is prepared properly in rehearsals, the students sing with confidence. If the director is prepared for all scenarios in a concert, everything will come across smoothly.[2]

Performance Attire Matters

When chorus members see each other dressed in something other than their normal school clothes, the performance takes on an air of importance and significance. Before they sing a word, they sense that this is a unique and special event. Given

---

[2] Pagel and Spevacek, 63.

plenty of notice and resources, children's choirs of all social strata can look like a unit of people who belong to each other.

I insist that our choir members arrive for performances with concert attire on. For us, it's black on the bottom half (slacks, not jeans; knee-length skirts are optional for the girls), black shoes, black socks, and white on top (dress shirts for the boys, blouses (not turtlenecks) for the girls). Ties are supplied for our boys and neck ribbons for the girls. In their black and white, they look like a chorus proud of its accomplishments.

I remember watching an elementary school "choir" (it was actually classrooms pooled together for a single event) perform at an evening concert involving choruses from different schools. Participants in the other groups dawned robes, tuxes, and black dresses while this group looked as though they'd not changed from their everyday school clothes. Before they sang a word, I was predisposed to believe their performance would be subpar given their casual attire. Their visual appearance dramatically affected my perception of how the group might sound long before a single note was heard, and I'm pretty sure I wasn't the only one in the audience who felt that way.

Dressing in a similar fashion does not need to be extravagant or illogical for kids 10, 11, and 12 years old, but it is an essential part of the choral experience for children. I would not expect parents to spend an inordinate amount of a family's budget to outfit their sons and daughters.

At Canyon Creek, we have developed a fairly efficient hand-me-down system, allowing boys to select slightly used dress slacks and dress shirts from a stack donated at the end of the previous performance season. We store blouses, skirts, even shoes that are perfectly usable. Our community has several thrift stores available, as well as shopping centers with bargains galore. Given these options, black slacks or skirts and white shirts are easily attained. The fellows tend to wear black shoes that can double as athletic sportswear, while the girls (who normally have adult-size feet by 6th grade) wear flats owned by an older female member of the household.

With online shopping, mass quantities of T-shirts, polo shirts, or vests may be purchased at reasonable prices. It's almost cheaper to purchase these items than to ask seamstresses in the school to sew them. A friend of mine directs a large children's chorus of 4th and 5th graders; her chorus wears red vests with dark slacks and a white shirt. On stage, they look fabulous. She mentioned the vests are reused each year, making their initial investment last more than a decade.

In addition to the visual image of students dressed alike, the common attire inspires students to understand that they *belong* to each other. They are a community. They have a common goal and purpose. They are no longer individuals simply attending an event. They have a clear goal and commitment to achieving a high standard of performance. Before they open their mouths, the students symbolically and outwardly bond together.

Equally vital is the attire of director. The outfit should suit the occasion. Normally, I wear a long black dress for our evening concert in December, while choosing black slacks and a jacket or tasteful top for our field trips. In March, my outfit will normally have a bit more color to it, but it remains a huge step above what I wear to school. Bartle included some fun limericks to shed light on this topic. This was my favorite:

There was a conductor from Stack
Who wore colorful things on her back,
Blue bows that were frilly,
Red sequins looked silly,
'Twould be better if she had worn black.[3]

A "Class Act" Mentality

There is absolutely no reason a children's chorus should misbehave when participating in a performance event. Simply because they are kids is not a reason to accept anything less than honorable and respectful behavior. If the director has done her job, students in the elementary choir demonstrate poise, confidence, focus, and the ability to control themselves in all settings and venues. If there is any concern that inappropriate behavior might occur, the director must be ready with appropriate actions and consequences.

This does not mean excitement isn't present! Performing is an exciting event and it would be ridiculous to not accept and anticipate a level of exuberance and energy. Knowing the difference between well-earned enthusiasm and behavior that is not favorable should be a task the leader of the group is adept at recognizing.

---

[3] Bartle, *Sound Advice,* 95.

Bottom line? Proper behavior is taught. Nothing is more important than having the chorus members display a class act before, during, and after public performances. Instructional steps on what to do, how to do it, when to do it, and why to do it are essential for success. Taking the time to teach children what performance etiquette looks like, sounds like, and feels like is part of the job: In the end, *nothing matters more.* If the chorus sounds great but behaves inappropriately, audiences will be turned off.

Tragically, an audience may assume that because elementary chorus members are "just kids" they should be given a lower standard of behavioral expectation. Wrong! Children have the capacity to do what is right, but they must *know* what is right to begin with. Given the casual nature of our society, students have fewer opportunities to experience quiet dignity and personal control than they did 20+ years ago. Students need practice, feedback, and routines to establish those behavioral qualities we deem vital.

When a children's chorus is in the public eye, we want the community at large to view them in a positive light. I remember taking a choral group to a large shopping area for a holiday performing opportunity. Before taking the stage, a woman approached me and asked if I was connected to the kids in white shirts and turquoise ties. Reading the expression on her face, I knew admitting my relationship to them was not going to lead to any positive news. Sure enough, a couple of our boys were heard using foul language in front her young children while riding the elevator. That single confrontation wore on my heart and mind the remainder of the day, making all performances less than enjoyable. She identified the boys and an apology was quickly issued. Those fellows did not perform with the group; rather, they sat with a chaperone and were not allowed on subsequent field trips: A loss for them, but a greater loss for the whole chorus.

I tell that story to current chorus members so that they understand the impact their actions have on each and every one of us. In preparing for performances chorus members hear me say, "It's no longer about you: It's about us, our school, our families, our community, and the reputation our district has throughout the region."

Specifically, before we engage in any public performances, students are given direct instruction and modeling in the following class-act scenarios:

- Accept compliments graciously. Practice saying, "Thank you, I'm glad you enjoyed it" while looking the individual in the eye. A good firm handshake is a plus.

- Excel as a courteous audience member when other groups are performing. Enter and exit the performing venue between songs and only in the case of an emergency. Eyes on the performers, mouth closed, applaud appropriately. If given an opportunity and it is well-earned, congratulate members of other choral groups.

- Treat the venue as an honored guest. Feet on the floor, inside voices used when performance is not going on, hands off materials that do not belong to you, appreciation shown to our hosts.

- Remain focused and quiet on the risers and in the hall. Visiting with each other during performances (ours or another group's) is not acceptable.

- If a reception occurs after the concert, invite your parents, siblings, and other guests to move ahead of you in the line. Thank those who provide service; if you see a napkin or big crumb on the floor, pick it up and throw it away.

- Walk while in your concert attire. Running is not needed and not accepted. Moving confidently and in a controlled manner signals self-discipline and provides those watching that you know what you are doing and are aware of how you appear to others.

- Words carry weight—think hard before saying something that might come across as offensive or undignified. If a qualified adult (an audience member, chaperone, or school personnel) asks you to be quiet, or suggests you change what you are saying, do so. No questions, no backtalk. Do it immediately.

Rehearsal time is limited and while practicing the music is of paramount importance, practicing personal skills to employ in public has a longer lasting effect. I truly think elementary students like to be viewed in a positive way: They also enjoy the freedom that comes with a director's confidence in their actions. No one can relax and enjoy a performance when the behavior of a few kids causes negative distraction. Taking the time to teach what students can do to be a class act is well worth it.

Organization! Before, During, and After Performances

Swears wrote:

> Performances should be a natural outgrowth of the choral learning experience. A healthy student attitude to be developed throughout chorus rehearsals might be: "We have studied and worked hard to create the most beautiful music possible. Now it is time to share our music with others." Children do not respond favorably to last-minute rush or confusion. Try to avoid throwing things together at the last minute. No matter how hard your children have worked or how beautifully they sing, haphazard pre-concert preparation may result in a performance far below your students' ability and your expectations.[4]

Organizing the sequence of events that leads to quality performances is a process. Beyond the selection and instruction of repertoire, behind-the-scenes acts led by the director help the group look their best, sound their best, and behave their best. Beyond these benefits, the director and students can actually relax and enjoy the performance season, knowing that systems were activated in advance to help the group function in a productive manner.

---

[4] Swears, 174.

Being organized leads to smooth performances. It also creates a positive impression of the director among administrators and parents. Trust and faith is built when others see the students representing their school and families in a manner that befits a purposeful, respectful, and well-intentioned young person.

Check the List; Check It Twice

Beyond the preparation of repertoire and behavior, the director has several organizational chores to check off prior to performances. For a non-field trip-oriented performance, the director needs to:

- Secure performance venues
- Select, reserve, and publicize performance dates with parents and school personnel
- Put together a program that includes selected repertoire, the accompanist's name and student names, information about the choral or music program at the school, and acknowledgements of those who've helped the group be successful (parent or staff volunteers, the school administrator, etc).[5]

---

[5] A copy of the program for our December concert, portions of which are shown throughout the performance chapter of the DVD, is provided at the end of this chapter. Note that the students' names have been omitted for reasons of privacy and safety.

- Communicate with personnel at the venues to be sure necessary equipment is accessible and ready (risers, piano, piano bench, music stands, solo mics, etc.)
- Organize non-chorus volunteers to distribute programs, help seat late arrivals, set up any chairs, tables, or the like that are required for audience comfort

Swears wrote:

When children have worked hard and prepared their music well, it is important for them to have performance experiences. These performances should provide a learning experience for students and a service or benefit to others… Special performances must be worked out in detail and should come at times that enhance the overall choral schedule.[6]

Off-campus performances are great fun and provide an excellent opportunity for the chorus to participate in community outreach. However, the director must be very thorough in planning the field trip experience for the chorus. In part, the director should:

---

[6] Swears, 180.

- Secure transportation
- Distribute and collect permission slips
- Secure a sufficient number of qualified chaperones
- Confer with the school office staff, especially the nurse (more students than ever have particular medical requirements that become the responsibility of the director when away from school)
- Prepare information packets for drivers and chaperones, with information of the day's events and locations
- Prepare a checklist of what students need to bring (coats? food?)

Further organizational questions to consider are:

- How will the trip be financed?
- What food options are needed? If students bring a lunch, what should be included and where will they eat it? If students are buying food, be sure to converse with them and chaperones about appropriate choices.
- Do students understand the expectations and consequences for behavior?
- What will students do when they are not performing?

- Is the environment secure, safe, and appropriate for elementary-age children?
- Do students have a grasp of who will be in the audience and what the setting might look like? (For instance, if singing at a children's hospital or an elderly care center, having a sense of the environment is extremely helpful.)

Even with the best organization possible, things happen: Students must understand that flexibility is key. I distinctly remember a field trip when maintaining flexibility and accommodating surprise events were essential. The trip began with a solid rainstorm—the kind of rain Seattle does not normally see (we have drizzle for nine months, but not too many "pouring rain" episodes). On this day, the rain was drenching. We began our first concert with dripping hair and attire; one girl twisted her ankle as she bounded across a puddle. Fortunately, her mom was a chaperone and was able to purchase an Ace bandage for her. Once wrapped, her ankle improved throughout the day.

My shoes were very slippery and at a key moment in one of the selections, I stepped back rather suddenly, slipped on the heel of my shoe and promptly fell off the stage. My right elbow hit the floor hard as the rest of me landed soundly into poinsettia plants sitting on the floor. I spent the remainder of the day conducting with my left arm as my right elbow swelled. That was our morning.

In the afternoon, one girl had a nosebleed that wouldn't stop. She happened to be one of our soloists. One of the boys had a severe asthma attack requiring paramedics. This occurred shortly after one of the fellows fell flat on his face, having fainted. Although I saw the guy white-faced and slumping, my own discomfort with my arm was paramount on my mind. When a student whispered, "Mrs. Bourne! Mrs. Bourne! I think Nathan just died! Mrs. Bourne! Nathan is down and isn't getting up" my thoughts were jarred loose and help was called over. Later, it was interesting to listen to a recording of our performance and hear this fellow's desperate whispers while the chorus happily sang "Holly Jolly Christmas." It wasn't such a holly jolly experience for Nathan, for me, for the girl with the ankle, the boy with asthma, or the girl with the nosebleed, not to mention the kids who still had wet clothes chilling them.

Despite everything that occurred on that field trip, prior organization made up for the disasters that ensued. Adequate chaperones and staff were there to help, transportation proved reliable, we didn't lose a single child, and the "day of disasters" was something we could laugh about...after a few months. The kids remained flexible and took everything in stride. I was immensely proud of them, but knew that pre-field trip organization could be credited for the good things that ultimately occurred that day.

Pagel and Spevacek wrote:

> Nothing can topple your stature as a chorus teacher or your program's reputation more than a performance that looks unorganized and unprepared. When the director looks scatter-brained or the students look dazed and confused, there can only be one person held responsible—the director....Looking and sounding your best doesn't mean that everything will go off without a hitch—that's the magic of a live performance. However, the things that are under the control of those involved should be as prepared as possible.[7]

During the big-push phase of rehearsals (the last few before showtime) I begin previewing, in my own mind, what I want chorus members to look like, sound like, and feel like the evening of our first concert. If I'm well organized, the kids

---

[7] Pagel and Spevacek, 63.

know where to go once they arrive. They know the sequence of events that will occur that evening; they know where they will sit, where they will stand, the order of music, and how they will find their families once the evening concludes. Everything that can be predicted is covered in rehearsals. I describe what the performance venue looks like (if located beyond our school gymnasium) and what they will see from the stage. My goal is to leave nothing to chance, knowing that things happen and that we'll all go with the flow!

Enhancing the Performance

Beyond the basics of performance—the dates, the venues, the performance attire, the starts and stops, the behavior and demeanor of choristers—the director might consider inviting an additional music group to perform as invited guests. For the past several years, our high school has graciously accepted an invitation to perform during our holiday concert in December.

Not only does a guest group's performance expand the evening's entertainment, it also expands the audience base. Depending on who is invited, additional performers bring along additional listeners. As long as the venue can accommodate the increased numbers, inviting another group (particularly one with older performers) can be a very positive learning opportunity for the elementary-age student.

The evening is enhanced through the performance of our high school students. They exude the qualities I'm trying to inspire in my students: graciousness; professionalism; arriving ready and organized, polished and prepared; positive on- and off-stage demeanor; appreciative of the opportunity to share their music. Our elementary parents are able to watch these young adults with full knowledge that the choral-ensemble experience is not an isolated experience at Canyon Creek.

The evening program is also enhanced with the help of our building administrator, who becomes our master of ceremonies. He greets the audience, reminds them to turn off cell phones and silence pagers. He asks for appropriate performance etiquette—quieting young children, leaving and entering the venue between songs, keeping feet on the floor. It would seem adults should know these things, but this kind of formal concert experience is new for some families. They want to do the right thing and normally appreciate the manner in which our principal coaches them on audience etiquette.

Having the elementary school administrator intimately involved in the performance sends a message to everyone: He cares about its existence, understands the quality the organization is trying to attain and maintain, and supports the professional atmosphere we are trying to create. Parents see him tying ties, directing parents where to drop off students, helping clean up the reception area. On stage and off, his presence is appreciated.

I've attended concerts where the building principal was not present. That too communicates a message to parents and community members. Although there may be extenuating circumstances, it seems peculiar to not see a building principal attend an elementary performance event that celebrates weeks and months of rehearsals. I do remember one incredible performance that occurred without our principal in the audience. Although the group sang beautifully and the audience of music educators (at a state conference) offered a standing ovation, her absence was sorely felt by all, especially me.

Beyond enhancing the performance with those who might appear on the stage, a reception for chorus members and their families is a positive way to celebrate the first performance of the year. Parent volunteers supply the food and the set-up, while chorus members enjoy the fellowship and fun that awaits them after the concert. Seeing families together, watching girls receive flower bouquets from parents, talking with

younger siblings who can't wait for their turn to be in chorus, taking pictures with members—it's a great way to reap the rewards of hard work.

I believe one of the primary goals of establishing and maintaining a successful children's chorus is to sing quality music in quality performances. Quality performances will occur if the students are well rehearsed, sufficiently groomed, and adequately prepared for their time in the spotlight.

Elementary students have the capacity to share both musicianship and citizenship, if steps lead toward those ends. Having watched groups whose behavior casts a negative light on the director, I have chosen to go to extremes to prevent that from occurring. As one of my chorus member's parents indicated, "I really don't know how you do it! I have ten of those boys on the baseball team I coach and I know how hard it is to get them to focus for more than five minutes!"

Teaching kids how to behave has become part of the job for elementary educators. It's not a bad thing, it's not a good thing—it's just reality. Through the choral experience, students learn skills they will use the rest of their lives that go far beyond the repertoire and the concert halls. Performances offer opportunities for kids to prove to everyone how very capable they are, musically and behaviorally.

Boonshaft wrote:

> We don't just teach music, we teach excellence in everything through music. Our purpose is to help young people find happiness in their lives. To experience heights of emotion and thrills of success. To understand that through excellence in doing anything comes the reward of its virtues.[8]

Performances offer an opportunity for students to reap the benefits of hard work. They provide a setting where emotions, exuberance, and excellence blend together. They offer the public an opportunity to glance inside the elementary student's realm of possibilities. By the time students take the stage, the director can and should look upon her members as highly capable musicians and citizens.

Take the time to teach performance etiquette. Your students are worth it.

---

[8] Boonshaft, 172.

Canyon Creek Chorus

 Holiday **C**oncert

Northshore Performing Arts Center

Welcome
Bill Bagnall, Principal, Canyon Creek

Special Guests:
The Bothell High School Jazz Choir and the Bothell High School Men's Choir
Directed by Mrs. Sheri Erickson

Canyon Creek 5th/6th-Grade Chorus
Directed by Patricia Bourne, Accompanied by Yuh-Pey Lin

"Hava Na Shira"   **Hebrew round**
Translation: "Let Us Sing Together: Sing Alleluia"

"Ayelevi"   **Traditional song from Ghana**
with "BorBorBor" drumming, as arranged by Master Drummer Sowah Mensah
    A song of life and celebration
        Solo Call:
        Drum Ensemble:

"The Journey"   **arr. Joseph Martin**
The melodies of this beautiful piece are taken from Dvorak's Symphony in
E minor and the Shaker tune "Simple Gifts"

"I'll Be Home for Christmas"   **Gannon/Kent, arr. A. Beck and A. Naplan**
        Drumset:

"Watu Wote"   **Sally Albrecht and Jay Althouse**
In Swahili, "Watu Wote" means "All the People." Additional words heard
include "imbiana" (sing together), "wimbo etu" (come hear our song), "si, si
sote" (all of us belong)

"Gloria"   **David Giardiniere**
Performed in traditional Latin, based on a traditional text of the church from
the 14th century and beyond

"Children Go Where I Send Thee"   **arr. Ruth Elaine Schram**

"Christmas Is Coming and We Are Getting Fat!"   **Dave and Jean Perry**
        Soloists:

"Walkin' in a Winter Wonderland"   **J. Bernard**

Many Thanks

A huge thank you to all of the parents of chorus members—your help and
support mean the difference between this group existing and not. To the
Canyon Creek staff—Mr. Mayberry, for the use of the gym during rehearsals;
Mrs. Pomranz and Mrs. Pennington, for answering questions, helping with
everything and anything; Mrs. Ford, Mrs. Jennings, Mr. Booth, Mrs. Brenden,
Mrs. Peterson, Mrs. Hansen, and Mrs. Anderson, for delivering messages
to students, encouraging participation, and magnificent support of this
afterschool experience; Mr. Bagnall, for serving as "master of ceremony" and
supreme supporter of the Canyon Creek Chorus; Mrs. Erickson and the choral
ensembles of Bothell High School—thanks for being a part of our concert on
your home turf; finally, a thanks to Yuh-Pey Lin, our accompanist. You have
given our group a chance to perform musically and with confidence. We are
indebted to you.

Future Chorus Dates to keep in mind…

December 11   Performances at Canyon Creek (9:00 A.M.),
                        with invited guests, the SVJH Choral Ensembles
                Winterfest (Seattle Center, 1:15)
January 9   First rehearsal of 2008
March 11   Concert (with BHS, CPJH, SVJH)
March 12   Chorus celebration; end of performing season

 Happy Holidays!

Final Thoughts

Going inside the elementary chorus reveals multiple levels of instructional, personal, and musical dynamics to consider. Deciding to offer chorus within the elementary school can be exceedingly worthwhile to all involved; however, to do it well requires the heart, mind, and soul of a committed director.

The director of a non-select elementary chorus learns to recognize and value the unlimited vocal potential of her students. She sees and hears what is vocally apparent on day one, but has the ultimate sound desired in her mind. Directors of

elementary choirs employ strategic instructional steps to lead students from what is to what it can and should be.

Listening to and watching children's choruses perform can be an experience that inspires the most sophisticated of audiences. For those who are unaware of the musical abilities of children, the sound of a well-coached elementary choral ensemble comes as a remarkable surprise. It's particularly inspiring to learn that the children one sees and hears have been accepted into the choir regardless of vocal ability.

I'm grateful to have an opportunity to direct a non-select elementary children's chorus. I'm thankful to my colleagues for their support, the parents of my students who demonstrate faith and trust in me as director, and my building administrator for championing the group.

My greatest thanks go to the students who've elected to spend an additional hour and 15 minutes pursuing choral excellence. It has been, and continues to be, one of the greatest privileges of my professional life.

As Bartle wrote:

Next to effective parenting, teaching children is perhaps the most important job in the world. Teaching children to sing, and to sing well in a fine choir, is work that embraces far more than actual singing. We mold lives. We teach values. We develop tastes. We inspire and nurture talent and creativity. Each of us must continually strive to improve our skills, our craft, and our knowledge of great music making.[1]

My ultimate goal for the elementary children's choir boils down to one word: Appreciation. Appreciation for each other, appreciation for the art form, appreciation for the ways we can create community through quality experiences, appreciation for the opportunity to learn in an authentic, highly visible manner, appreciation for unique beauty.

I live and work around people who develop an appreciation for life. I simply can't imagine a better career than that.

---

[1] Bartle, *Sound Advice*, 4.

Appendix: Recommended Repertoire

Additional Recommended Octavos: Heritage Music Press

For General Concert or Contest Use

Title	Composer	Catalog #	Voicing
Ahrirang	arr. Brad Printz	15/1534H	2-part
American Folk Rhapsody	arr. Linda Spevacek	15/1213H	2-part
And This Shall Be for Music	Mary Lynn Lightfoot	15/2479H	2-part
Cantate Deo (from *Water Music Suite*)	Handel/arr. Mayo	15/2162H	2-part
Cantate Hodie! (Sing Today)	Mary Lynn Lightfoot	15/2090H	SSA
Chumbara	Dave and Jean Perry	15/1548H	2-part
Dona Nobis Pacem	Mary Lynn Lightfoot	15/1175H	2-part
Dreams that Children Dream	Ruth Elaine Schram and Celsie Staggers	15/2224H	2-part
Drinking Gourd, The	arr. André J. Thomas	15/1564H	2-part
A Festive Alleluia	Mary Lynn Lightfoot	15/1417H	SSA
Hi Ho! The Rattlin' Bog	arr. Linda Spevacek	15/1536H	2-part
How Beautiful is the Rain!	Mary Lynn Lightfoot	15/1272H	2-part
I Hear America Singing	André J. Thomas	15/1655H	2-part
If I Could Catch a Rainbow	Brad Printz	15/1538H	2-part
Inscription of Hope	Z. Randall Stroope	15/1081H	2-part
Ja-Da	arr. Linda Spevacek	15/1392H	2-part
Joshua Fit the Battle of Jericho	arr. Brad Printz	15/1348H	2-part
Kang Ding Flower Song	arr. Victor C. Johnson	15/1827H	2-part
Painless Opera (Opera non Terrore)	Phyllis Wolfe White	15/1448H	Unison/2-part
The River Sleeps Beneath the Sky	Mary Lynn Lightfoot	15/1306H	SSA
Sing for Joy! (Duet from the oratorio *Judas Maccabaeus*)	Handel/arr. Spevacek	15/1286H	2-part
Something Told the Wild Geese	Sherri Porterfield	H5890	2-part
Woke Up This Morning (Freedom Song)	arr. Cynthia Gray	15/1848H	2-part
Casey Jones	Russell L. Robinson	15/2463H	2-part
This Train!	Russell L. Robinson	15/2303H	2-part

For Christmas, Holiday or Winter Performances

Beautiful December	Amy F. Bernon	15/2537H	SSA
Christmas...In About Three Minutes	arr. Mark Weston	15/1537H	2-part
A Holiday Hand Jive	Greg Gilpin	15/1367H	2-part
Lullay Alleluia	Ruth Elaine Schram	15/2418H	SSA
On This Still, Silent Night (*Still, Still, Still* and *Silent Night*)	arr. Laura Farnell	15/2004H	2-part
Riu, Riu, Chiu	arr. Linda Spevacek	15/1415H	2-part
Winterlight	Amy F. Bernon	15/1883H	2-part

Choral Collections for Elementary Choirs: Heritage Music Press

In Concert! Distinctive Repertoire for Two-part Choirs (45/1109H)
Compiled by Mary Lynn Lightfoot
Performance/Accompaniment CD (99/1640H)

Sing for Joy! (from Judas Maccabaeus*)*	Handel/Linda Spevacek
Joshua Fit the Battle of Jericho	arr. Brad Printz
Where Do the Stars Go?	Sherri Porterfield
Jubilate Deo	Mary Lynn Lightfoot
Haru Ga Kita (Spring Has Come)	arr. Greg Gilpin
Ja-Da	Bob Carlton/Linda Spevacek
Sanctus	Schubert/Donald Moore
America, the Free	Phyllis Wolfe White
Inscription of Hope	Z. Randall Stroope

Singable Solutions for Winter Holidays: Eleven Creative Two-part Treble Settings (45/1131H)
Compiled by Mary Lynn Lightfoot
Accompaniment CD (99/1817H)

Sing a Glad Noel!	Mary Lynn Lightfoot
Pat-a-pan	arr. Greg Gilpin
Silent Night	arr. Earlene Rentz
Calypso Noel	Linda Spevacek
Mistletoe	Phyllis Wolfe White
One Word	Linda Spevacek
Whatcha Gonna Call That Baby?	Phyllis Wolfe White
A Holiday Hand Jive	Greg Gilpin
Sing with Joy, Sing Noel! (Personent Hodie)	arr. Brad Printz
The Candles of Hanukkah	Amy F. Bernon
Winter Sleigh Ride	Cynthia Gray

We Sing the World Around: A Multicultural Journey (45/1145H)
Compiled by Mary Lynn Lightfoot
Accompaniment CD (99/2132H)

Farewell, My Friend (Africa)	Ruth Elaine Schram
Chumbara (France)	Dave and Jean Perry
Zum Gali Gali (Israel)	Greg Gilpin
Haru Ga Kita (Japan)	Greg Gilpin
Ahrirang (Korea)	Brad Printz
Three Pacific Island Lullabies	Linda Spevacek
(Phillipines, Hawaii, Tahiti)	
De Colores (Spain)	Mark Weston
Chíu, Chíu, Chíu (Uruguay)	Greg Gilpin

Winterscape: Seasonal Selections for Two-part Treble Choirs (45/1155H)
Compiled by Mary Lynn Lightfoot
Accompaniment CD (99/2306H)

Let's Take Sleigh Ride!	Mark Weston
Winterlight	Amy F. Bernon
First Footprints	Phyllis Wolfe White/Karen Bodoin
Something Told the Wild Geese	Sherri Porterfield
In Winter	Rebecca Rossiter
A Winter Wish	Dave and Jean Perry

Song Collections and Musical Reviews: Heritage Music Press

All of the following include reproducible vocal parts, narrations, and a performance/accompaniment CD.

Pictures of December, by Greg Gilpin (30/2112H)
It's Christmas Everywhere!, by Ruth Elaine Schram (30/2360H)
For Which It Stands, by Greg Gilpin (30/2222H)
Ten Who Counted, by Greg Gilpin (30/2361H)
The Words We Live By: Creative Songs Teaching Historical Words That Shape Our Lives, by Greg Gilpin (30/2041H)

Additional Octavo Selections: Miscellaneous Publishers

Title	Composer	Publisher	Catalog #	Voicing
Al Shlosha D'Varim	Allan Naplan	Boosey &Hawkes	1358866	SA
Cameroon	Musuka/arr. Scott	Alfred	00-SV9533	2-part
Can You Hear Me?	Bob Chilcott	Oxford University Press	3183191	2-part
Catch The Spirit, Feel the Magic	David Maddux	Alliance	AMP0469	SA
A Child of Song	Herring/Beck	Alfred	00-23539	2-part
Ding, Dong Merrily on High	arr. Herrington/ Glick	Pavane	P1102	2-part
Gloria Tibi	Leonard Bernstein	Boosey & Hawkes	OC266344	SS, w/ T solo
Haida	arr. Henry Leck	Plymouth	5303532	Unison
Hope for Resolution	Caldwell/Ivory	earthsongs	W-34	2- or 3-part Treble
It Don't Mean a Thing (If It Ain't Got That Swing)	Ellington/arr. Emerson	Hal Leonard	08551780	2-part
The Journey	Joseph M. Martin	Shawnee Press	E0361	2-part Mixed
Look at the World	John Rutter	Hinshaw Music, Inc.	HMC1527	Unison
The Moon	Andy Beck	Alfred	00-28541	2-part
Old Joe Clark	arr. Herrington/ Glick	Pavane	P1017	2-part
Path to the Moon	Eric H. Thiman	Boosey & Hawkes	OCTB6114	Unison
Sahayta	Ben Allaway	Shawnee Press	YS0510	SSA
Song for a Pirate Child	Vijay Singh	BriLee Music Publishing Co.	BL125	2-part
Song for the Mira	MacGillvray/ Calvert	Gordon V. Thompson	1663798	SSA
South African Suite	arr. Henry Leck	Plymouth	1863687	SAB
Winds	Larysa Kuzmenko	Boosey & Hawkes	OCTB6833	SS

Bibliography and Selected Resources

Bartle, Jean Ashworth. *Lifeline For Children's Choir Directors.* Toronto: Gordon V. Thompson Publishing Corporation, 1988.

Bartle, Jean Ashworth. *Sound Advice: Becoming a Better Children's Choir Director.* New York: Oxford University Press, 2003.

Beam, Douglas. "Respecting the Voice: Four Music Teachers Discuss the Challenges of Teaching Children to Sing." *The Orff Echo* 15 (summer 2008).

Bennett, Peggy. "So, Why Sol-Mi?" *Music Educators Journal* 91, no. 3 (January 2005): 43–49.

Bennett, Peggy and Douglas Bartholomew. *Songworks I: Singing in the Education of Children.* Belmont, CA: Wadsworth Publishing, 1997.

Boonshaft, Peter. *Teaching Music with Passion: Conducting, Rehearsing, and Inspiring.* Galesville, MD: Meredith Music Publications, 2002.

Bourne, Patricia A. *Inside the Music Classroom: Teaching the Art with Heart.* Dayton, OH: Heritage Music Press, 2007.

Bourne, Patricia A. "Instructional Techniques for Children's Choirs." Ed.D. diss., Arizona State University, 1990.

Bresler, Liora. "Music and the intellect: Perspectives, interpretations, and implications for Education." *Phi Delta Kappan* 87, no. 1 (September 2005): 24–31.

Broeker, Angela. "An Interview with Six Successful Elementary Choir Directors." *Choral Journal* 45 no. 10 (April 2006).

Campbell, Patricia Shehan and Carol Scott-Kassner. *Music in Childhood: From Preschool through the Elementary Grades.* New York: Schirmer Books, 1995.

Ehly, Eph. *Hogey's Journey.* Dayton, OH: Heritage Music Press, 2006.

Eklund, Peter A. "25 Tips for Engaging Male Singers." *Choral Director* 1, no. 2 (winter 2004) 10–14.

Esquith, Rafe. *Teach Like Your Hair's on Fire: The Methods and Madness Inside Room 56.* New York: Viking Publishing, 2007.

Gackle, Lynne. "Selecting Choral Literature for Children's Choir, a Closer Look at the Process." *Choral Journal* 47, no. 5 (November 2006).

Given, Barbara K. *Teaching to the Brain's Natural Learning Systems.* Alexandria, VA: Association for Supervision & Curriculum Development, 2002.

Goetze, Mary. "The Children's Choir: An Ideal Setting for a Musical Education." Paper presented at the Washington Music Educators Conference, Yakima, Washington, February 2008.

Gregoryk, Joan. "Choral Music Education Begins in the Classroom." *Choral Journal* 46, no. 10 (April 2006).

Gruwell, Erin, ed. *The Gigantic Book of Teachers' Wisdom.* New York: Skyhorse Publishing, 2007.

Gumm, Alan. *Music Teaching Style: Moving Beyond Tradition.* Galesville, MD: Meredith Music Publications, 2003.

Herrington, Judith. "Mission Possible – Children Can Sing Beautifully." Paper presented at the ArtsTime Conference, Tukwila, Washington, March 2003.

Johnson, LouAnne. *Teaching Outside the Box: How to Grab Your Students by Their Brains.* San Francisco: Jossey-Bass, 2005.

Kodály, Zoltan. *The Selected Writings.* New York: Boosey & Hawkes, 1974.

Lautzenheiser, Tim. *Everyday Wisdom for Inspired Teaching.* Chicago: GIA Publications, Inc., 2006.

Marshall, Herbert D. "Elementary Choir Resources." *General Music Today* 18, no. 2 (2005).

Marshall, Herbert D. "Elementary Choir Resources." *General Music Today* 20, no. 2 (2007): 34–38.

McCord, Kimberly and Emily H. Watts. "Collaboration and Access for our Children: Music Education and Special Educators Together." *Music Educators Journal* 92, no. 4 (2006): 26–33.

McRae, Shirley W. *Directing the Children's Choir: A Comprehensive Resource.* New York: Schirmer Books, 1991.

Mizener, Charlotte. "Our Singing Children: Developing Singing Accuracy." *General Music Today* 21, no. 3 (spring 2008): 18–24.

Neu, Terry W. and Rich Weinfeld. *Helping Boys Succeed in School.* Waco, TX: Prufrock Press, Inc., 2007.

Pagel, Randy and Linda Spevacek. *The Choral Director's Guide to Sanity...and Success!* Dayton, OH: Heritage Music Press, 2004.

Parker, Elizabeth Cassidy. "Intrapersonal and Interpersonal Growth in the School Chorus." *Choral Journal* 48, no. 2 (September 2007): 27–31.

Phillips, Kenneth H. *Teaching Kids to Sing*. New York: Schirmer Books, 1996.

Rao, Doreen. *The Children's Chorus: On Location with the Glen Ellyn Children's Chorus*. American Choral Directors Association, 1988. Videocassette.

Rao, Doreen. *We Will Sing: Choral Music Experience for Classroom Choirs*. New York: Boosey & Hawkes, 1993.

Rottsolk, Rebecca. "Rehearsal Techniques: The Responsibility of the Conductor." Paper presented at the American Choral Directors Association Inservice, Seattle, WA, October 2003.

Schmid, Will. *World Music Drumming*. Milwaukee: Hal Leonard Corporation, 1998.

Scott, Julie. "Singing in the Schulwerk: What are its Roles and Importance?" *The Orff Echo* 15 (spring 2008).

Small, Ann. "Beginning a Children's Choir: No Dinosaurs Here." *Choral Journal* 47, no. 2 (August 2006).

Smith, Janice. "Every Child a Singer: Techniques for Assisting Developing Singers." *Music Educators Journal* 93, no. 2 (November 2006): 28–34.

Sprick, Randy, et al. *The Safe and Civil Schools Series: Proactive, Positive, and Instructional Discipline*. Eugene, OR: Safe and Civil Schools, 2005. CD-ROM.

Stafford, Douglas. "Perceptions of Competencies and Preparation Needed for Guiding Young Singers in Elementary School Music Classes." DMA diss., The Florida State University, 1987.

Stultz, Marie. *Innocent Sounds Book I: The Singer's Journey Begins—Building Choral Tone and Artistry in Your Children's Choir, Book I*. St. Louis: Morning Star Music Publishers, 2007.

Stupple, Caroline. "The Male Changing Voice: The Student's Experience." *Teaching Music* 15, no. 1 (August 2007): 36–44.

Sullo, Robert A. *The Inspiring Teacher: New Beginnings for the 21st Century.* Washington D.C.: National Education Association, 1999.

Swears, Linda. *Teaching the Elementary School Chorus.* West Nyack, NY: Parker Publishing, 1985.

Trollinger, Valerie. "Pediatric Vocal Development and Voice Science: Implications for Teaching Singing." *General Music Today* 20, no. 3 (spring 2007): 19–25.

About the Author

Patricia Bourne teaches K–6 general music, 5th/6th-grade chorus, and a 6th-grade marimba ensemble at Canyon Creek Elementary in Bothell, Washington. Prior to this, she was Coordinator of Music Education at Central Washington University, in Ellensburg, WA. A veteran music educator of 28 years, Patty is active as a workshop presenter, guest conductor, and secondary vocal adjudicator. This is Patty's second book published with Heritage Music Press.

Patty received the Bachelor of Music Education from Murray State University, Murray, Kentucky, followed four years later with a Master of Music Education degree from the University of Oklahoma, Norman, OK. In 1990, she completed the Doctorate of Education (Ed.D.) from Arizona State University, in Tempe, AZ.

Beyond her fulltime teaching position, Patty contributes editorials, articles, and lessons for *Activate!*, a general music education magazine published by Heritage Music Press. She is a featured clinician with JW Pepper, presenting workshops and leading choral reading sessions at conferences throughout the country. During the summer, Patty maintains an active schedule as presenter and teacher for the World Music Drumming workshops.

Patty, her husband, Tom, and daughters Katherine and Julie reside in Bothell, Washington.

Credits for
Inside the Elementary
School Chorus DVD

AYELEVI
With BorBorBor drumming of Ghana,
    as taught by master drummer Sowah Mensah
Used by Permission

CHILDREN, GO WHERE I SEND THEE
Traditional Spiritual
Arranged by RUTH ELAINE SCHRAM
© 1998 STUDIO P/R
All Rights Controlled and Administered by
    ALFRED PUBLISHING CO., INC.
All Rights Reserved   Used by Permission
www.alfred.com   Alfred #SV98135

CHRISTMAS IS COMING AND WE ARE GETTING FAT
Words and Music by JEAN AND DAVE PERRY
© 2001 HERITAGE MUSIC PRESS, a division of
    The Lorenz Corporation
All Rights Reserved   Used by Permission
www.lorenz.com   Lorenz #15/1627H

GLORIA
Words and Music by DAVID GIARDINIERE
© 2006 HERITAGE MUSIC PRESS, a division of
    The Lorenz Corporation
All Rights Reserved   Used by Permission
www.lorenz.com   Lorenz #15/2200H

THE JOURNEY
Arranged by Joseph M. Martin
© 2005 Malcolm Music, a division of Shawnee Press, Inc.
All Rights Reserved   Used by Permission
www.shawneepress.com   Shawnee Press # E0548

PEACE SONG (WITH WE SHALL OVERCOME)
Words and Music by GREG GILPIN
© 2005 HERITAGE MUSIC PRESS, a division of
    The Lorenz Corporation
All Rights Reserved   Used by Permission
www.lorenz.com   Lorenz #15/2008H

WATU WOTE (ALL THE PEOPLE)
Words and Music by SALLY ALBRECHT and JAY ALTHOUSE
© 2005 ALFRED PUBLISHING CO., INC.
All Rights Reserved   Used by Permission
www.alfred.com   Alfred #23607

Produced by Puget Sound Educational Television, a
    cooperative of Puget Sound Educational Service District
www.psesd.org

Videographer and Producer: Bruce Fisher,
                                Fisher Video Productions
Producer: Kerry MacDonald

Special thanks to:
    4th-, 5th-, and 6th-grade students
    Canyon Creek Elementary
    Bill Bagnall, Principal
    Northshore School District

    Yuh-Pey Lin, Accompanist

DVD Contents

Classroom Techniques
Active Engagement
Posture/Breath Support
Pitch Matching
Music Reading Skills
Articulation, Resonance, Clarity of Text
Conducting Gesture, Expressive Singing
Interpretation of Repertoire

Choral Rehearsal
Establish Routines & Warm-ups
Articulation, Intonation, Tone
Rhythm, Meter, Form, Pitch, Style

Performance
Pre-Concert Warm Up
Hava Na Shira
Ayelevi
The Journey, by Joseph M. Martin
Watu Wote (All the People), by Sally Albrecht and
    Jay Althouse
Gloria, by David Giardiniere
Children, Go Where I Send Thee, arr. by Ruth Elaine Schram
Christmas Is Coming and We Are Getting Fat,
    by Dave and Jean Perry